Ted Bailey

A MAJOR SOLDIER

To Frank, Ernest and Edgar
and all the soldiers of Essex

Ted Bailey

A MAJOR SOLDIER

Reveille
PRESS

Reveille Press is an imprint of
Tommies Guides Military Booksellers & Publishers
Menin House
13 Hunloke Avenue
Eastbourne
East Sussex
BN22 8UL
www.tommiesguides.co.uk

First published in Great Britain by
Reveille Press 2011
For more information please visit
www.reveillepress.com

A catalogue record for this book is available from the
British Library

ISBN 978-1-908336-20-0

Cover design by Reveille Press

Typeset by Graham Hales

Printed and bound in Great Britain by
CPI Antony Rowe, Chippenham and Eastbourne

Contents

Pictures

Natalie Adams – 27
John W. Burrows – 22, 24
Essex Regiment Museum (FGB Thomas Collection) – 21
Colin Green, MRICS, per Essex Regiment Museum – 29, 35
Hilder Family, per Essex Regiment Museum – 54
www.1418.net.maps – 38, 39
www.commonswikipedia.com – 28, 43
www.diggerhistory.info/ – 25

www.enwikipedia.org – 5
www.firstworldwar.com – 23
www.iwm.collections.com – 40, 41, 45
www.schools-wikipedia.org/ – 9
www.upload.wikipedia.org/ – 42
www.wereldoorlog.1418.nl/ – 37
www.worldwar1photos.com – 18, 19, 20, 26, 31, 50, 51

Abbreviations

The following abbreviations appear in this book and the Appendices:
AA: Anti Aircraft (colloquially: Ack Ack)
ASC: Army Service Corps
BEF: British Expeditionary Force (Western Front)
Bde: Brigade
Bn: Battalion
Capt: Captain
C-in-C: Commander -in-Chief
Col: Colonel
Cpl: Corporal
CO: Commander Officer
DCM: Distinguished Conduct Medal
Div: Division
DOW: Died of Wounds
ERG: Essex Regiment Gazette
ERM: Essex Regiment Museum
GOC: General Officer Commanding
HQ: Headquarters
ITC: Infantry Training Centre
IRA: Irish Republican Army
IWM: Imperial War Museum
KIA: Killed in Action
L-Cpl: Lance Corporal
Lieut/Lt: Lieutenant (also as prefix to Colonel and General)
MEF: Mediterranean Expeditionary Force (Gallipoli)
MI/MIC: Mounted Infantry/Mounted Infantry Company
MM: Military Medal
MOD: Ministry of Defence
NCO: Non Commissioned Officer
QM: Quartermaster
RAMC: Royal Army Medical Corps
RAOC: Royal Army Ordinance Corps
Regt: Regiment
RFA: Royal Field Artillery

RFC: Royal Flying Corps
RSM: Regimental Sergeant Major
Sgt: Sergeant
TNA: The National Archive
V1/V2: Victory Rockets (German)
VC: Victoria Cross
WIA: Wounded in Action
WO1: Warrant Officer Class 1
WW1: World War One

Acknowledgements

A VENTURE such as a search into an ancestor's life and the consequent writing of a book is never conducted single-handedly. I received much guidance and help which, without exception, has exceeded my expectations. I have been consistently gratified by the lengths that the people consulted have gone to in providing me with assistance and also surprised by their genuine interest in what I was doing. I wish to acknowledge the invaluable contributions from the people mentioned below who played a key part in this project and without whom it would have been a much harder task.

I particularly wish to thank Ian Hook, the Keeper of the Essex Regiment Museum, for his prompt replies to all my enquiries and for a constant flow of crucial information which considerably extended the search with some surprising results.

Thanks are also due to: Keith Sellars and Owen Tuckett for their reading of the first draft; Jane Carter, serendipitously discovered as the owner of the Bailey Family Tree and great granddaughter of Ernest, grandad's elder battalion brother who provided me with vital data and photographs; Ernest's elder daughter Doris for some family insights; Joe Firmin, the grandson of Frank's eldest sister who also extended family connections; Darren Tansley for organising the earlier edition and finally, Ann who motivated and supported me throughout.

Introduction

THIS IS the story of my grandad, Major Frank Bailey, who left a small rural community and spent over thirty five years as a soldier in the Essex Regiment and was directly involved in all the major battles of World War One (WW1). It is about youth and ageing: my youth in his ageing and his youth in my ageing. It is the fond memory of my early years with him which, inspired later by sheer chance and an intense curiosity, really opened up the door to his hitherto unknown life. It turned out that, as well as being a professional soldier, he was nothing less than a quiet hero.

My discovery of grandad's unsung heroism was indirectly triggered by two coincidences which, although they occurred at different times, for me came together to create a personal 'big bang'. The first was my younger son, Nicholas, asking for any information about his great grandad's WW1 involvement for a school Remembrance Week project and my inability to find much first-hand material. The second was catching a television documentary that made a passing mention of the Essex Regiment at Gallipoli, something I did not know. If they were there, was grandad Frank?

Trawling the WW1 websites revealed little data about the Essex although many other soldiers featured in relatives' eulogies. I could only vaguely recall my granny's many kitchen anecdotes about their army travels in the colonies but the war was never mentioned. Grandad certainly never uttered a single word about it. To my regret, I realised I knew little or nothing about him as a soldier and hoped it was not too late to find out. The time had come to uncover this mystery once and for all. I owed to myself and my sons. Now completely hooked, I embarked on a full detective search.

This book is the result of that search through a vast array of records and sources to unravel and record all available details of my grandad's army life.

Inevitably, chasing the tale of someone's life from a bygone age led to many highs and lows but both were stimulating in their own way. A lot of time was spent in a state of anxious limbo waiting for responses to enquiries that seemed to take forever to appear. Then there were the sudden and totally unexpected revelations that blew the trail wide open.

What emerged was nothing short of stunning and filled me with pride. There was a surprising subplot. Two of Frank's elder brothers were also in the army, one in the same battalion and the other in a different unit, killed in 1917 and buried near Ypres. I started out with a specific focus on Frank but having discovered the brothers I now felt the need to include them in a larger picture which encompassed a more mixed bag: part family story, part regimental eulogy and part battle and army history.

The last two aspects help to provide some background for the reader unfamiliar with matters military. The changing nature of the British Army is explained to show what kind of organisation Frank joined and how his final promotion as Major was still, even by then, a very remarkable social feat for a rural lad from a tiny Essex village.

Clearly the army made him, turning him from a farmer's boy into a military man, from an unskilled worker into a qualified horseman and sharpshooter, from a quiet man at home into an inspiring leader and hero on the battlefield.

The story of Frank and the 1st Battalion Essex Regiment are inseparable: the battalion shaped him and he helped shape the battalion both in war and peace. It is right to recognise and honour Frank, his brothers and the brave Essex comrades and their immense contribution beyond the county in foreign battles.

The 1st Essex was at Gallipoli, The Somme and the long trail from Arras to Cambrai in 1917. These names thunder out to us from the past even now as dreadful reminders of the immeasurable carnage wreaked upon a whole generation of idealistic young men who were sacrificed in that most grotesque war. The history of these battles is a well-trodden trail but it is fitting they merit a brief revisit as background to the contribution of the 1st Essex. All information is as accurate as the evidence available but the background comments are all mine based on inexpert reading.

Although it is not an adventure story as such I employ the present tense to capture the feelings and fears of the soldiers when in action. The past tense is more properly used when describing or analysing the history of campaigns and general events.

Pictures and maps are referred to at the appropriate point in the text and presented together centrally. Some of these images date from WW1 so every possible effort has been made to enhance their definition. Where necessary, to avoid interrupting the flow, explanatory notes appear at the end of each chapter and all details of cited sources are listed at the end for those wishing to follow them up.

Finally, I grew up in the fifties in a Europe untouched by 'hot' war. For this I am grateful and hope our descendants in turn also appreciate living in peace. During this investigation my grandson was born on the morning of 11th November 2007, a date I will not forget.

Ted Bailey, 2008

I completed the original narrative of Frank and his brothers over two years ago but knew there were many more facts that remained undiscovered. Since then though, more relevant information has come to light and this later data has been incorporated into this edition. Nevertheless the search continues.

Ted Bailey, 2010

1.

My Grandad: A Quiet Man

Wartime memories

I'm in the dark. I'm lying on my back looking upwards. There's a rumbling sound. Suddenly there's a loud thudding noise close to me. Something is falling onto me. I can't breathe. A man rushes in. He grabs me, scoops me up in a cloth and pulls me away. Now, in his arms and wrapped up in this cloth I feel us moving very fast in a downwards motion. There's a light on somewhere. I'm being swept along with a rushing feeling and then, suddenly, I feel cold air swirling around us. I feel cold and am back in the dark. Now there's a dim light again and I'm inside a damp building.

That paragraph sums up in words my earliest ever infant memory. It's visual. That's exactly how I remember it although I didn't then have the words to describe it like that until I was much older. It occurred over 65 years ago but I still recall it vividly to this day. I realise that the whole thing can only have lasted a minute at the most but the image is sharply defined and permanently imprinted in my brain.

A German plane had crashed and exploded nearby. That was the rumbling noise while the thud was a bit of it landing on our roof. In my cot upstairs I was exposed to the collapsing ceiling which disintegrated into little pieces of plaster revealing its trelliswork underbelly in a cloud of choking dust. I was covered in it. I can still see the trellis pattern now.

The man who rescued me was my grandad Frank. He had rushed in, grabbed me and swept me away to safety. At the moment of the impact he sprinted upstairs, scooped me up in my eiderdown and ran downstairs out into the garden and into the Anderson Shelter. There was no warning siren. It was a returning plane. My grandad saved my life. He stopped a Nazi bomber getting me before my first birthday. From then on he was a big influence in my life. He was inherently quick thinking and a brave man. This I never realised until much later in life.

Much as I would love to I have never been able to pinpoint the exact date of this incident. My granny used to tell me many stories and this was one. Today I could kick myself with frustration for not making a note of the details of that earliest event. What I do remember is being told it was sometime during the Blitz and our house, not for the only time, was hit by a passing bomb. The Blitz lasted until May 1941 when the Germans diverted their attention to invading the Soviet Union so although it sounds very unlikely it does mean this happened in my first year of life. Amazing!

When writing this chapter I looked up psychological work on early infant memories. Without delving into that subject at irrelevant length I did discover two very interesting facts. First, recalling memories before two years of age is regarded as rare and some believe impossible. Second, these memories are regarded as 'episodic' being encoded and stored in a purely visual mode as we do not yet have verbal language to express them.

However, more relevant to my situation is that an emotionally or physically traumatic event can imprint itself in our stored memory before we can talk and be recalled verbally later on. My earliest memory was certainly traumatic. It is visually seared into my mental wiring. Even now, I can see that image as it happened all those years ago and describe it as above but in no way do the words capture the real impact of that memory.

My grandparents corroborated this and some other early wartime events when I was a bit older. Obviously, being told when I was more able to understand provided me with a verbal frame to hang the image on. They also told me when it happened but unfortunately I cannot recall that time aspect in contrast to the image itself. However, I always believed that this occurred before my first birthday.

I was born in 1940 at the end of air battle over the skies of Britain and during the night-time Blitz over London. I lived with my grandparents and my aunt in Brentwood, Essex just 21 miles from the capital. I lived with them because my parents had separated shortly after my birth and my father was serving out in the Far East.

We lived in a detached house (Picture 1, next page, with later extension) which was halfway down a tree lined residential drive which at one end fed into thickly wooded countryside and another road that led a couple of miles to where my grandad's Essex Regiment had their Warley Headquarters. Pre-

1. *The house in South Drive*

war it was the sort of place where peace and quiet prevailed but now it lay directly under the main Luftwaffe bombing route to London, from occupied Belgium and Holland.

Our area suffered much damage because German pilots often dropped unused bombs on their way home and also some incoming pilots panicked over fierce local heavy anti-aircraft barrages doing the same and heading straight home. The terrifying wailing of the air raid warning sirens were a constant backlog to our lives and it is an intense sound that insinuated itself deep into my consciousness and in my memory.

As a matter of official record, over 1,000 bombs were dropped on Brentwood, with 19 doodlebugs, 32 V2 rockets, many incendiary bombs and parachute mines and this resulted in 5,038 houses destroyed, 389 people injured and 43 dead. Two of those events were ours. Ironically, at the start of the war in September 1939 alone over 6,000 London children were evacuated to the area because it was considered to be safe enough!

I was told we were "bombed out" twice during the war. I have never known whether that meant a direct hit or a nearby explosion that damaged the house. I've since discovered that a Dornier 17 bomber was shot down there on 16th January 1941. Given my first memory, it is still spine chilling to think that despite his best efforts, Hitler didn't manage to get me even before I could walk. In 1942 the Luftwaffe began low level lightning 'hit and run' strafing and bombing raids on Essex airfields, railways and factories.

The local RAF airfields at nearby Hornchurch and North Weald were key targets. Strangely, unlike my earliest memory these later raids have not registered with me at all even though I was two.

They tried again in 1944 with the notorious V1s or 'doodlebugs'. I clearly recall those with intuitive dread. They had a distinctively low rumbling sound rather like a modern diesel engine as they crossed the sky. Then, there was the terrifying moment when the engines cut out. The deep silence that followed before the inevitable explosion was like waiting for a huge thunder clap that follows lightning. The nearer the silence the more dangerous it was to be underneath. You took cover and froze. Ask anyone who lived through their reign of terror and they will tell you the same thing.

I also saw 'gold and silver planes in the sky' most likely through some gap in our shelter. We left an opening because the floors in those things were always damp or waterlogged. Like First World War trenches, duckboards were a must. Grandad said they were enemy planes caught in the searchlights of the local anti-aircraft batteries. Coincidentally, that image is like the searchlights in the current logo of the Imperial War Museum. I also clearly remember throwing half-a-dozen eggs from of my pram outside the front of the house. Naturally, I was told I was not at all popular for some time after given strict wartime rationing!

Peace Arrives

One fairly fine day grandad grabbed me by the hand and said we were going out. I was excited because I always loved going out with him. We walked down South Drive turned left and down the hill hand in hand towards the bridge that crossed the London and North Eastern Railway line. He was taking me to the 'Seven Arches Pub'.

This was the nearest one to our house on the way into the town. The bar was bedecked with loads of those little coloured triangular flags. He propped me up on the counter in the left hand corner of the bar where I sat with a soft drink and watched a right royal shindig. He was chatting animatedly to some other men. All the men and women were shouting and drinking. There was much laughter, kissing, and dancing about. Clearly to my young eyes something important was going on it and it was very exciting and enjoyable. It turned out to be 8th May 1945: VE Day, the end of war with Germany and an occasion for communal relief and celebration.

A similar party occurred in September not in the same place but somewhere in a nearby road. This was to celebrate Victory over Japan and the absolute end of the war. Little did I know then that these were mileposts of world history: key chapters in making the world into which I was entering and would later study.

These are the most vivid wartime memories that have stuck in my mind to this day. My inability to recall anything more specific is apparently the result of what is known as 'childhood amnesia', ironically the exact opposite my earliest graphic memory. This is a confusing contradiction, between being able to recall some events and not others. Despite the war and its obvious dangers, clearly oblivious to me for the most part, I do generally recollect those times with my grandparents as exciting, secure and happy. Somehow it was always sunny although this perception is impossibly silly. I do remember grandad with great affection because he always took time with me and as I got older I realised he had a mischievous sense of humour which greatly appealed to me.

Growing up with grandad

Our house in South Drive had a big sprawling garden and grandad grew a wide variety of vegetables. Contemporary knowledge says private gardens were converted to fully functioning allotments because fresh produce was almost impossible to buy and everyone followed the 'Dig for Victory' policy. In the summer months, a large plot of tall cabbages, potatoes, rhubarb and other vegetables formed an ideal playground for games of cowboys and Indians and hide and seek with a couple of neighbourhood friends. Each row of plants was raised leaving a handy dip in between providing cover for hiding and sniping. At the end of the garden my grandad also grew runner beans of a size that belies even adult belief and the cane structure formed a superb camouflage from the imaginary enemy.

We were allowed to hide in this foliage provided we did not damage the precious vegetables. However, young boys being boisterous and distracted grandad was often ticking us off for our errant trampling. He always did so in a quiet way whilst explaining why we shouldn't do it. Looking back now on that time he always seemed to have a slight smile playing at his mouth and yet there was an aura of stillness and calm dignity that surrounded him. He somehow seemed to be elsewhere with his thoughts.

Very often he would come outside and sit sunning himself in a wicker chair overlooking his vegetables and have a quiet smoke. I remember a strange ritual when he was smoking. As he exhaled he would stroke back and forth under his chin with his hand. When I first smoked I copied this believing it to be the sign of a real smoker. I equated it with women lifting one leg when kissing in the Hollywood movies. Needless to say I soon learnt that both these were unnecessary to these activities.

In those moments he would be far away in his own world of thoughts as if in a trance. I now realise this was most likely the result of his war experiences. Between 1914 and 1918 he was involved first hand in all the major campaigns and scenes of the most awful death and destruction. He also recently had a small indirect part in the second war as the officer trainer for local anti-aircraft batteries.

One day, a stranger in a khaki uniform just appeared in the back garden and said "Hello". This was my father back from the Far East. Obviously, I hadn't a clue who he was. To me he was anybody. It must have been very difficult for him seeing me for the first time in over four years now no longer an infant. Once inside the house there was a noisy commotion and everyone was happy. Some neighbours came round and it felt like yet another party.

This was clearly a landmark in my life but somehow it passed me by. The significance was wasted on me: a five year old more interested in playing outside. I was always intensely involved in the imaginary games and other activities often to the exclusion of much of what was going on around me.

That winter of 1946-47 was famous in the annals of weather. It was one of the coldest in recorded history and the country was struggling with post-war recovery. Rationing was strict, there were shortages of everything and it always seemed to be cold except in our front room where my granny always put up a roaring fire. We amused ourselves with continual snow fights and sledging down the road in the local wood. South Drive was on a bus route and single-decker buses used to stop near our house. They were like those charabancs you now see in the Agatha Christie reruns.

One day there was much excitement in our otherwise quiet suburban drive when there was deep freezing snow covering the whole area. One of these coaches got stuck at the stop near our house and could not move away. The wheels started spinning furiously chucking up snow all over the place and eventually all of us, kids included, had to help dig it out of the snow drift and push it with much difficulty along the road to a firmer spot. We loved it. It was out of the ordinary routine and made our day.

In the spring of 1947 we suddenly moved to Ongar Road on the other side of town. I have no clue as to why. At this time my aunt moved out and got married so maybe that was why. Even to this day I still don't really know. Apparently, grandad was never interested in owning a house but was content to rent. I suspect this was in his bones from his many army postings. Granny hated this and regularly berated him for not wanting to settle down. It was a slightly smaller house so maybe they were saving on the rent now my aunt was no longer living with us. The garden was just as big though and in no time it seemed that grandad's runner beans and tomatoes were sprouting up healthily. Ironically, the house we moved to was a few doors down the road from where I was born during an air-raid.

In the September of the same year, aged nearly seven, I was sent away to a boarding school in Surrey. My granny's Catholicism required a religious education and apparently all the RC schools in Essex had been obliterated during the war. Well, that was her reason but I suspect it was not totally true. That first half-term was a very lonely time and I was very homesick and lost as if in a void. I couldn't wait for the break to come round to see the reassuring smile of my grandad and be secure at home.

In the Ongar Road house there was a long kitchen leading into a scullery and on into the garden. In an alcove in there was one of those anthracite boilers, a bit like modern wood burning stoves which was constantly alight to provide hot water. It gave out a great deal of comforting heat.

When home from school, I particularly treasured what I can only describe as a warm 'weekend feeling.' Grandad had the papers delivered and over breakfast at the weekends would scour them wearing his glasses, one side

stuck with plaster and looking very serious. After he had eaten, he would disappear to the front room or 'drawing room' they called it. He used to get 'Reynolds News', 'Daily Sketch' (both now defunct) and the 'Sunday People'. I also remember a magazine called 'Tit-Bits' which also folded.

Picture 2 captures the true nature of the man, sat by the radio, or 'wireless' as it was called in those days with the newspaper

2. *Grandad in his favourite armchair*

in his favourite armchair. I took it in 1955 a year before he died. He looks just like a typical grandad with the silver hair and clipped moustache that makes him look distinguished. The regimental tie hints at his past that remained locked away. His kindly reassuring smile and twinkle in the eyes hints at that sense of humour.

He always listened to the nine o'clock evening news on the then BBC Home Service and while that was on he would not brook any distractions and we had to be very quiet. I found this ritual comforting and welcomed it more as I got older. At home with them was definitely one of my most happy and stable experiences.

He was like the silent but strong captain of a ship: the home-ship away from school. Around him I always felt reassured as I tucked into my granny's fried bacon, egg and tomato breakfasts which were something else. Today I can still capture that unsurpassable taste of those salty tomatoes, very memorable and far superior to those found in the supermarkets of today.

'Elephant in the Kitchen'

Whilst growing up, much time passed spent in the kitchen listening to my granny's wide variety of anecdotes about their army travels together abroad. India was clearly a big theme and better appreciated having read Kipling and also studying foreign history at school. Although always fascinating they were disparately dotted about here and there so there was no clear pattern in my easily distracted young mind. Perhaps because of their transient nature they did not remain uppermost in my mind for very long fading into a cloudlike background.

As a term time boarder I was now only home for the main school holidays and so there was not as much time available to hear these tales or to ask about them. Youth is about the immediate present so what was the point of banging on about the past? More important peer group activities at school gabbed my attention particularly my recent development as a good athlete. Of course, as an adult, I regret that loss of interest.

Over time those isolated bits and pieces of these exciting army stories began to form a vague sort of silhouette in my mind. I felt I wanted, in fact needed, to know far more about grandad's army experiences. What facts did I know then? I knew he had been in the army and had travelled widely abroad. He had also been in the Great War. This was the most tantalising part but was never mentioned. It resolutely remained the elephant in our kitchen.

It was extremely exciting that this man had been in a real war. Young boys seek adventure and imagining warfare the way it was in comics I was itching to find out all I could about what grandad did in the war. I hoped against hope he would tell me fascinating stories about his wartime deeds when I was old enough. He never did.

I guess deep down I really knew he would not discuss it under any circumstances but despite this my curiosity often got the better of me. When I was studying school history, I did venture to ask him the inevitable question. Sometimes when I thought the time was ripe I sneakily tried to trick him into it but clearly my attempts were never clever enough. Yes, there was always India but never any details about the war to feed my craving for tales of heroic deeds. Surely this was some kind of conspiracy? I should have pushed my luck more but somehow did not dare. Thinking back, I would not have got anywhere anyway.

Despite the history lessons, in my immaturity I failed to grasp the true significance of this immense part of our national story or the part his generation played in it. Of course, it is easy looking back with adult hindsight to see that those diverse snippets are actually the family narrative that reflects those larger events. Too bad my youthful distraction typically proved to become the 'if only I knew then what I know now' syndrome.

It was my growing up which initially led to a deeper understanding of his obvious reluctance to speak of that terrible war. This silence was like a tangible barrier preventing any memory from breaking out. Of course it was literally a mental block. What our grandfathers and great uncles witnessed and suffered in the spring of their youth in that awful war, the so-called 'war to end all wars' was nothing short of horrendous. The Great War, with its adjective valid only in the sense of gigantic, was a monstrosity and a gross blight on the face of humanity. Its true meaning to those involved can never ever be matched by mere description.

The survivors of that destroyed generation could never bring themselves, even briefly, to recall those terrible sights and sounds let alone talk about them. When you actually stop to think about what happened to them it is no surprise. So many of their mates failed to even make it through the first hours of engagements and in the long run the Allies paid a dreadful price for the final victory. Grandad was extremely lucky to have survived that indescribable experience for the whole four years and looking back now I realise the lasting and corrosive effect it had on him. No wonder he was someone who said very little in the way of small talk or casual conversation.

Life in Ongar Road carried on normally and the much anticipated school

3. Tea in the garden

summer holidays seemed to be a ceaseless sequence of long languorous days that seemed to last forever. When the weather was fine, and it did always seem to be sunny, we always had mid-afternoon tea in the garden, another welcome ritual, shown in Picture 3. Granny doted on me continually producing many delicious things to eat and drink and grandad entertained me with his special brand of wit.

It was in my sixteenth year. The spring term was just under way when I got the news. Grandad was very ill. He was in hospital and I had to go home to visit him immediately. I travelled across London fearing the worst. When I saw him in Harold Wood Hospital he seemed just the same as ever although a lot thinner and I fancied a little subdued.

We were pleased to see each other and had a good chat. Unknown to me he was dying and it was kept from me. I do remember overhearing a whispered comment that his condition was partly the result of being gassed in the trenches which struck me as odd. I had not known that. I was surprised that the effects could last this long.

I returned to school the next day and settled back into the routine. My grandad died a few days later. The news was given to me by a teacher. I was utterly devastated. I felt I was adrift in a dark cavernous space. This was the first time I experienced anyone dying. He was a heavy smoker in his early years like most of his generation but otherwise he was extremely fit for a man of his age. After all he was only seventy odd which is nothing in these modern times.

On my return home for the funeral I discovered his coffin in the aisle of Brentwood Cathedral. I saw it virtually 'lying in state' draped by the Union flag with his officer's cap and sword on top. I was simultaneously amazed, confused and emotional. He had been my big friendly, quiet and very funny grandad. He had been my special mischievous buddy. We had shared a sense of enjoyment particularly delighting in sneakily laughing at my grandmother's sometimes erratic behaviour. He was altogether a very special man but now he was gone. The bond was no more than a sad memory. I have the warmest memories of him to this day.

As to the regalia in the church it was all part of a military funeral. At the graveyard, as his coffin was lowered into the ground, they played the 'Last Post'. It was intensely moving. Manfully for my years I vainly fought back the tears choking on my emotions but in the end they won out.

Ironically, after he died my grandmother told me two significant facts about his wartime exploits. He had been gassed in the trenches and had won a gallantry medal by capturing a German pillbox and taking seven prisoners. This was a massive shift from the vague anecdotes and it gave them a more distinct form. Finally, I had a secret never revealed and this new knowledge filled me with reflected pride. Surely there must be more? In time, I would eventually discover how special this man with the calm exterior actually was.

Inevitably life imposes its day-to-day demands, even after a family death and for me it was straight back to school and studying for exams. Now my favourite subject history intrigued me even more than before and my zeal for it fed directly into my desire to know more about the Great War. Strangely though this did not immediately translate into specifically finding out about my grandad's part in it.

Exams and leaving school came and went and I embraced going away to college and working hard on my now burgeoning athletics career. From time to time, one or two jogs to this 'grandad memory' occurred although they still did not produce any action. This was particularly true with the adoption of colourful Victorian dress uniforms by some young people as a cultural style in the mid-sixties. Needless to say this caused much harrumphing and complaints to the media by some old soldiers.

This potentially strong nod to military matters should have reminded me about grandad's army career but shamefully, at least in my own terms, it did not trigger any renewed interest. It was fairly quickly forgotten in the miasma of the creative music and happenings that characterised that period.

Was this a subconscious hint to chase up his record with my father or aunt? Most likely it was but I did not respond to it being too busy pursuing other things with my own family and career. This was a very long time before the recently increased interest into genealogy.

A Missed Opportunity!

I got on well with my recently widowed aunt who lived nearby. She had been my surrogate mother when the real one left me with my grandparents in my first year. In my mid-twenties we were out one day having lunch together in a local restaurant when she suddenly asked: "Do you know anything about your family? Did they ever tell you what happened?"

"No", I did not. I confessed I knew virtually nothing and that I had put it to the back of my mind. She was amazed at my response and expressed outrage at this lack of family communication. On returning home and over much more wine she was clearly keen to tell all. Now, I was all ears. All of my family past tumbled out in a nonstop flow of consciousness: everything, including juicy skeletons from the proverbial cupboard about my granny, my parent's marriage, my birth, their separation and my father's immediate posting to Burma. I even discovered an interesting tale about my father turning down a chance to become an officer. He had been in the Territorial Army before the last war and was apparently offered a regular commission in 1939 but refused it. Later he was called up and posted to the Far East as a Private. Why remains a mystery.

As this river of hitherto unknown information flowed over me I was riveted. The trouble was the wine infusion. Listening is one thing. Remembering and recalling later is another. The next day I could only remember very few details in a vague story. Having not made any record of this highly significant conversation within a few days it was virtually dust.

2.

Chasing the Soldier's Tale

A S SAID in the previous chapter, when growing up all I knew about my grandad Frank's army career was only what was gleaned from my grandmother who made me aware of his service abroad as a regular soldier with her playing a leading role in his rise to officer status and peppering them with exotic Indian words, such as: 'buckshee', 'dekko', 'jildi' and 'pukka'. However, this was little more than a disparate collection of anecdotes and so never really attained any real logical hold in my memory. Not that this mattered to a young mind filled with Kipling's 'Kim', *Boy's Own Paper* and the *Eagle* because like their adventure stories hers all sounded very exciting and, anyway, an exciting story is a good story regardless. I lapped them all up.

As I got older, I did wonder about her self-appointed role as the driving force behind grandad's promotion through the ranks. Surely, I reasoned, he must have had some small part in his own progress. My aunt later confirmed that she did have a partial role when they were in India but that was not at all unusual in colonial postings where the wives were important mainstays of the entertainment whirl. We often joked about this and agreed that being Irish she obviously had a 'touch of the Blarney'. [1]

On leaving home for college these snippets of the grandad story faded into the cellar of my mind as I inevitably became more concerned with my own affairs. Not only that, but during the sixties our eulogised colonial past was subject to radical and jolting revision and reappraisal particularly fuelled by the escalating Vietnam War. I had dismally failed to seize the opportunity presented by my aunt to record the family narrative. When I eventually wanted to get information to write this I found there was no clear outline at all. All I had was this set of disjointed anecdotes just skimpily hanging together. I had the gravy but not the beef.

There was a vivid exception though and it related to a specific wartime incident. After he died I discovered that Frank had stormed and captured a German pillbox and taken its seven occupants prisoner. I was mightily impressed with this heroism from the man I had known as mute on that subject. This was obviously what the gallantry medal was for. I was so proud of him. Strangely, this incident was to be reprised but in a different form later when I was chasing facts about his career.

Two coincidences combined to trigger a strong desire to find out all I could about his army life. The first was when my younger son asked me for any information and/or souvenirs showing any direct family involvement in the Great War as part of his school GCSE project.

Apart from a photo of grandad Frank as a Major in full uniform displaying many medals and the specific medal citation for bravery, which for the life of me I could not find, all I could offer him was the sum of the kitchen stories. This was that his great grandad was in the Essex Regiment, fought in the Boer War, was posted to India, Burma and Mauritius and served in the Great War. He was awarded the Distinguished Conduct Medal (DCM), was gassed and eventually retired as a Major.

That was it: a bald statement of a whole 36 year career which in no way captured a rich life in all its complexity.

That would have been that but for the surprise intervention of a television documentary on Gallipoli which made a passing but significant mention of Essex Regiment involvement with a couple of soldier's descendants visiting the battlefield area. My mind began to buzz. Immediately, the obvious question: if the Essex was there, was grandad Frank there too? I trawled the internet for WW1 websites for any possible data about him or his regiment. The results were both confusing and frustrating but also moving. Countless postings of soldiers and their war deeds by relatives, tributes to individual soldiers killed in action, some from Essex but many more from other units regaled me. Mostly though, entries on the Essex Regiment were frustratingly thin on the pages and there was not a single mention of Frank Bailey.

If the Essex Regiment was at Gallipoli I had to chase up this singular and tempting fact. I decided there and then I would undertake a detailed investigation on all possible fronts to pinpoint Frank's active military career and put substance onto the skeletal knowledge inherited from my youth.

What follows is a brief summary of the main aspects of the process and progress of that search.

To complement it, I post a record of it in diary form (*Appendix A*) which shows things as exactly when and how they occurred and written up en route. It is an authentic record. I have only used people's first names to preserve their identity except where it has been otherwise agreed. It is not a clearly unfolding sequence but rather a series of disparately interrupted stops and starts. A detective story springs to mind. There are many helpful books giving well-organised information for these army service and ancestry searches but I did not refer to any until well under way.[2]

Often, investigations are written up as if there was a clear sequence to the events when there was not any. We humans like tidiness and it is tempting to do this in hindsight. Of course, a more systematic search might have yielded results more quickly from the outset or maybe not. Mine developed in its own intuitive meandering way and I am glad of it.

To start with it was a bit of a scattergun approach but in time things began to coalesce into some ordered shape. At times I actually enjoyed the feeling of confusion and apprehension that preceded a possible discovery. Sometimes chaotic and often routine it was always an all-consuming and exciting experience savouring the many problems of access and picking my own inimitable way through the morass of fascinating information. The quest itself has proved as rewarding as the outcome. At the outset I had little if any real substance to work on. Even now, the story still leaves some annoying gaps. Despite its idiosyncratic nature I hope my dairy will act as a rough guide for anyone else who wants to pursue this type of enquiry.

* * * * * * *

On the 'starting line' a friend, looking to find her long lost father, gave me a tip that proved invaluable. It was a superb flying start and saved me much time and effort scrabbling round to work out how to get going. Every regiment has its records and artefacts stored in some museum. "Start there" she said. I contacted the Essex Regiment Museum (ERM) and the Keeper, Ian Hook (IH) was immediately very helpful by sending me their computerised data base of Frank's service. That document was a factual but bare outline of the what, when and where but no more than that. Nevertheless, it was a big boost because for the first time I had some actual written evidence to work on.

This initial probe into Frank's army service revealed a distinguished service record over many years and a gallant soldier in action against the enemy. Immediately, there was a big surprise. It was something very remarkable about which I had absolutely no idea. Frank was in the 1st Battalion, Essex Regiment and they had indeed landed at Gallipoli in the first hours at Cape Helles to reinforce another regiment. Coincidentally the documentary had pointed me to him being there.

As regards him being gassed I now had a date but still no location. Even though this and other facts appeared out of the paperwork I was hungry for many more details to better interpret them. For instance, how serious was the gassing? Did it leave a permanent consequence that may have revisited him in later life? The more I found out the more questions arose that beckoned me to push on further up the road.

Also, in his reply to me the ERM Keeper asked if Frank had a brother who was a Drum Major in the same regiment. I never remember grandad having any relatives at all, let alone brothers, so the answer was obviously "No". Little did I know then how wrong I would be and how delighted to be proved so.

This first attempt to gain information now began to mushroom uncontrollably into something far, far bigger than I could ever imagine. It was as if I was shifting a car into overdrive. As I pushed on, urgently following the trail with all its twists and turns, not only did my inquiry remove layer upon layer of Frank's army service but it also uncovered more juicy nuggets.

Gaining access to Frank's Ministry of Defence (MOD) Service Records provided both a fuller picture of his career but also another big surprise. Among the photocopies of enlistment details, a specific sequence of dates, postings and promotions was something that stopped me in my tracks. The

4. Extract from Military History Sheet

names of three older brothers: Joseph, Charles, and Ernest appeared as next-of-kin on the Military History Sheet and next to Ernest's name were the words "*Essex Regiment*"! (Picture 4)

An immediate phone call to the ERM produced a much appreciated exponential leap: Ernest turned out to be the very brother IH had recently inquired about. So after all, Frank did have a brother and not only in the same regiment but in the same battalion at the same time and engaged in the same campaigns. This was indeed a huge leap forward.

Another surprise was that Frank and, in the light of the new data, Ernest had not only been at Gallipoli on the first day of the action but they were also involved together at the Somme on 1st July 1916. The battalion had been involved on that fateful first morning at a place called Beaumont Hamel. Until then I had never even heard of Beaumont Hamel or knew where it was.

Sending off for Ernest's MOD records was imperative to round off the total picture of the battalion brothers. Not long after, the Census Records at The National Archive (TNA) threw up an extended family that even went beyond the three brothers mentioned in the MOD papers. There were two sisters and another four brothers, three of whom were older than Frank. Perhaps these brothers also served and maybe even in the same regiment? After all this searching and checking through of various data, there was now irrefutable written evidence that grandad Frank did belong to a large family and resulting from that, I too had inherited a large set of Victorian relatives, albeit dead.

Shortly afterwards, in trying to access further data on Frank's brothers from the Ancestry website, a fortuitous moment led to another amazing connection. A distant relative organising the Bailey Family Tree immediately responded to my inquiry and turned out to be the great granddaughter of Ernest! The whole family thing started rolling faster and faster. All my life until then, I never ever knew grandad had any family at all and, as far as I was concerned, my paternal grandparents were my only extended family.

I grew up with them in their home along with my father. My aunt was the only other relative. Typically, as a young child I must have accepted it as normal: the way things were. Growing older though, particularly during the school holidays, it did occasionally strike me as a bit odd that I was different from my friends because they had mothers and also a bigger array of grandparents and various other relatives.

When studying school history I realised that those born in the Victorian century almost inevitably belonged to large families and this trend continually reproduced itself between the generations. Strangely enough, this subject knowledge did not make any meaningful connection or impact upon my own lack of a large family so I did not seriously question why my grandparents apparently had no brothers or sisters. It is well known that most of us accept the daily routine of things at face value, subconsciously taking things for granted, because too much probing may disturb our settled view of the world.

With the benefit of hindsight and looking back on that period of growing up with them I assumed that there must be some explanation for the lack of any visible relatives. Families grow apart, get married and move about geographically. They lose touch. My grandad travelled widely with the army for many years and so maybe his lack of a permanent address for any length of time made contact difficult. Perhaps there had been a serious falling out in that family? In any case, it didn't bother me too much and by now I was busy getting on with my life at college away from home. I have since discovered that my grandmother did not get on with her in-laws at all so this explains the apparent lack of relatives and any remembered contact with them.

****

Relatives are also valuable resources in their own right. Sadly though, mine were all unavailable. Grandad Frank died when I was fifteen. He was never a great talker. When he did say something he was very funny and witty and he often entertained me when secretly mocking my granny's regular ranting about his supposed faults from the kitchen. Along with that he exuded a quiet dignity and stillness that impressed me even before I fully understood it. She, on the other hand, was voluble on most subjects hence the army anecdotes.

There are several problems in tracing someone's previous life, especially an army career that encompasses many different foreign campaigns that have long passed into history. Time is often the enemy of information. After all, these events in my grandfather's military career occurred in a frenetic world over ninety years ago and unfortunately the leading actor died over fifty years ago. Trying to put all these items together into some meaningful pattern after all that time is difficult but nevertheless necessary to my desire to create a suitably accurate interpretation of his life.

All we have left of a rich and varied life is a paper trail comprising a veritable maze of disparate documents many handwritten in illegible scripts. At least the copperplate style with its curly sweeps popular in those days, as in the extract, is generally easier to read but exactly deciphering many of these old documents is often compounded by incomprehensible abbreviations, particularly beloved of the army and also some dodgy spelling.

Access to first-hand documents such as a diary or letters are a huge boost in adding a unique personal insight. No such luck with Frank. Not only did he say little but as regards writing he was reticent to the point of reclusive. From my search he clearly never wrote anything down. There is no diary, no letters home so therefore nothing tangible to date. One of his nieces since confirmed this. This severely limited my quest, mainly restricting it to whatever documents *were* available.

Perhaps there are also some fading dog-eared sepia brown photos that we hope will tell us a story or teasingly reveal some scintilla from our ancestors' past. One such photo of grandad as an RSM has proved very informative (Picture 8). Some of these ageing photos can be considerably enhanced on computers and there are photographic shops that do this professionally.

Following the paper and photo trail may then lead us onto various gravestones and the many memorials that most places have or we can travel to the battlefield sites themselves. There we can photograph certain distinctive features and, whilst pausing to reflect, try to match the now quiet green fields in our imagination with what it was like for them under fire at the time. A digital camera proved invaluable.

Another problem arises. Back in grandad's youth working class people still only had a very basic education if any at all. Thus, when someone gave their name in the census or enlisted in the forces it was recorded as heard by the listener and how accurately they could write it down. Most had only the most basic writing skill and many areas also had strong local dialects. Pronunciation is the key here and a crucial name or place may be misheard, easily misinterpreted and so mistakenly recorded in writing for posterity. This was demonstrated where an Archive census return recorded Frank's brother Ernest as 'Arnest'.

Then there are the inevitable discrepancies between different sets of written records. How could these be resolved and establish which version is actually true? Expert advice says rely upon any data at the time of receipt and treat it as authentic unless it can be compared to something equivalent or which clearly supersedes it. That is all one can do because it was most likely recorded as accurate at that time.

An example of this was a discrepancy between Burrows' (1931) battalion history and MOD records. There was no way to satisfactorily resolve it. As a rule of thumb, unless a good reason not to, it is best to accept official records over unofficial and written over non-written data. However, Burrows is an authentically sourced and superbly detailed account with many first-hand inputs and proved invaluable because Frank's history mirrored that of his battalion. On the other hand, the MOD papers are the official service record relating to the individual concerned, so I have to go with this as the more authentic version.

Of course this is the major problem that dogs all research particularly combing through documents from the long distant past. Anyone who has ever done this type of search will immediately recognise the problems involved in seeking out and trawling through a complex array of primary and secondary sources dating back many years.

****

I started out on this trail with only what I could remember from those disparate stories via my grandmother. Initially, I was impatient to get the facts as quickly as possible and make a coherent story of grandad Frank and his army life. Things did not turn out like that.

It is a bit like an early morning mist. You fancy you can see various imperceptible shapes but are not so sure until the mist clears and the shapes become more defined and familiar. There were many false starts, dead ends and hurdles on the way, mostly overcome by dogged determination to get to the truth.

Although this was originally to be the story of my grandad Frank and his military career, untoward discoveries and events overtook it and out tumbled more facts especially about Ernest and another brother Edgar, whose army careers are briefly addressed elsewhere in a separate chapter.

What have I learned? With just a few second hand tales and some far from adequate facts, combined with persistence, occasional intuition and some contingent connections, I have largely uncovered the mystery of my grandad's life. This constant searching and chasing has now revealed the soldier's tale: a transformation from country boy to brave army man.

This challenging venture inducted me into a whole new world. It did so both gradually and suddenly but always enjoyably. This new world is a world of continuous revelation that has uncovered the life of a professional soldier in a previous age which shaped our modern history and still leaves its mark on our contemporary society. It has been said that the past is another country and this was a definitely the case here.

The final outcome reflects the disparate nature of a trail more convoluted than ever expected. Sometimes questions asked were answered quickly. At other times there were long periods spent tensely awaiting responses that stubbornly refused to appear. At least it seemed to be so given there was no timely response. Yet other inquiries drew complete blanks. One never knew though whether they would eventually yield up some information. At the time of writing there are still outstanding questions that remain.

I am indebted to Ian Hook who framed this apposite metaphor in describing this process of sending out a probe and waiting for its return. It is 'flash and bang', a military expression measuring the time lapse between ignition and explosion. Analogically speaking, a short flash and bang time is a prompt reply to a question. That is very gratifying and exhilarating and further intensifies the desire for more data. At other times you light 'the blue touch paper'- ask a question - and nothing happens for ages: no bang. Like a lit firework you worry about going near it in case it misfires. On yet other occasions you may have to relight it as I had to on occasion. Even now, I still await some big bangs with anticipation.

Anyway, any frustrating blips en-route have been totally outweighed by the sudden high of a lucky break, an unexpected discovery or contingent short-cut that inevitably accompanies this type of search. I have learnt to enjoy the whole experience of toying with a problem without necessarily having the solution immediately in sight.

I travelled on my journey of discovery as a wide-eyed tourist but also with a feeling of increasing excitement that came from the additional thrill of the explorer unearthing something intensely personal. There is the uncovering of grandad's heroic service and the unearthing of an hitherto unknown extended family. Both these discoveries are combined in the person of my grandfather: the soldier and the family member.

Also, something equally important has emerged. This whole venture has irrevocably altered my own sense of myself and my identity. I can now appreciate the powerful feelings engendered in those who engage in genealogical research and make untoward discoveries.

In this type of venture, authenticity is king. To be able to adequately verify the facts is the driving force behind such research. Obviously official documents such as MOD records are accurate from their time. Even then one has to double-check all details carefully to avoid discrepancies in them, such as seemingly different dates given for the same events or the apparent duplication of a promotion or posting.

Every effort was made to iron these out as far as possible to produce a satisfactory explanation. That is the nature of this enterprise.

I now have a more sharply defined picture of my grandad Frank Bailey, DCM, his army career and an elaborate narrative about his role in the Great War. This 'story' is outlined in more detail in the *Frank's War and Peace* chapter. It is complemented with an outline of the recorded events in his career, together with some inputs about his two military brothers and the activities of his battalion and their engagements (*Appendix B*).

NOTES

1. This means the speaker has the 'gift of the gab' having kissed the magical 'Blarney Stone' at Blarney Castle near Cork, Ireland.
2. *Army Service Records of the First World War*, by William Spencer is a useful resource for those wishing to trace relatives at The National Archive in Kew.

3.

The Changing British Army

MY GRANDFATHER Frank enlisted in the regular army aged eighteen in 1901, the same year that Queen Victoria died. He was the seventh of eight sons of a farmer, as shown on his birth certificate, although at this time this most surely meant farm labourer. Giving his occupation as a "barman", an unskilled working class occupation, he eventually worked his way up to become a Major by 1936. As occupational and social mobility in that historical period this was, by any standards, a meritorious and momentous career. Why so? Because at that time the British Army was still clearly rigid in its organisation: a distinct class-based dichotomy, divided between the officer class and the rest of the men.

In chasing up his military career many years after his death, I feel it important to identify what kind of army it was that he joined at the beginning of a new century. Taking a passing, if superficial, journey through its history helps to give some general background to the massive events that shaped his and millions of other soldiers' lives.

In 1901, the army was changing but far too slowly. It was still very much hidebound by tradition and those at the top were unwilling to change despite many pressures put upon them. Previous campaigns such as the Crimean War, 45 years before, where arrogance and incompetence at the top unnecessarily cost many lives and the then current second Boer War both amply demonstrated this. However, compared with our main political and economic rival, the German Empire, with its highly efficient conscripted army it was belatedly about to enter a period of rapid change forced upon it by technological advances in weaponry which was to produce a terrible new kind of warfare.

First though let us take a step or two backwards. There are two interrelated themes that fundamentally underwrote the structure of the British Army and gave it its essential character prior to its ultimate modernisation in the twentieth century. They are respectively the 'purchase system' that governed officers' commissions and the traditional temporary 'part-time amateur' basis of the army founded in the militia system. Like most aspects of the development of our society they were both rooted in the medieval period.

The Purchase System

Until well into the Great War of 1914-18, army officers were predominantly drawn from the upper reaches of society coming mainly from the landed aristocracy or gentry. These upper class sons were expected to be 'gentlemen' and sportsmen who had been educated at the great public schools which specifically prepared their charges for leadership and service in the far-flung colonial empire. In point of fact most of their time was spent engaged in social and leisure activities rather than actual soldiering.

This reflected a previous policy in operation up to 1871 where those wishing to be officers would to have to pay for their commissions directly to their intended regiment or through an agent acting on the behalf of the government.

The origins of this practice lay in the Norman feudal system whereby a landowner was required to provide knights for the king's service for 40 days a year. As time passed, money could be paid in lieu and this would be used to raise a force when needed, which in turn, became a system of granting individual commissions for a payment and the purchasing system was born. This informal arrangement continued in a haphazard fashion until instituted as a deliberate policy by Charles II for the creation of his small standing army on the Restoration of the monarchy after the Civil War.

It was the Duke of York's army reforms in 1796 during the Napoleonic War that regulated it by bringing in a number of explicit requirements for a person to become an officer. This was aimed at attracting men of fortune and character who were educated and would best know how to look after the nation's interest. They would most likely be following in the footsteps of their fathers or near relatives and thereafter take a step-by-step promotion up to the rank of Lieutenant Colonel (Lt Col). They had to be able to read and write and be of "good character" and vouched for by a senior officer. If they were dismissed from the army then they forfeited their payment.

These men had to be recruited from the right stock, or the right stuff, as we would say today. As they were predominantly upper class in origin and had bought their own commission, they had the most to lose from a revolution and so would have a selfish interest in guarding their financial stake by maintaining the status quo. This neatly supported the traditional English consensual climate of military independence from any possible dictatorship.

However, in 1809, the Duke of York had to resign because his mistress was trafficking in commissions! He was later reinstated when his successor proved to be inefficient. So it seems that the choice was between corruption and inefficiency. Either way, this practice led to the traditionally rigid attitudes that in turn produced a distinct lack of technical and tactical skill when it was needed in the battlefield.

In 1870, a young 'gentleman' could buy his Ensign's Commission, now Second Lieutenant (2nd Lt) for about £450-600 (comparatively £30,867-£41,156, by today's Retail Price Index measurement), a full Lieutenant rank (Lt) for about £700 (£48,000) in an infantry regiment and progress in promotion mostly by the Commanding Officer's (CO) recommendation. At each progression he would be expected to pay the difference between his previous and the next rank. It is interesting to note that the respective annual rates of pay were £27 (£1,850) and £41 (£2,812).

One exception to this was officers of the Royal Artillery and Royal Engineers who were properly trained and had graduated from the Royal Military Academy, Woolwich, but they were still regarded as "not quite gentlemen" by those gentlemen who had bought their rank! This academy, along with the Royal Military Academy, Sandhurst, was one of the only two proper training establishments at that time. Officers were not obliged to attend but those who did not attend optional formal training were prepared back at base by their regiments. They were required to train with the recruits until they were thoroughly proficient in individual drill and understood how to apply this by drilling a company of the men.

Those officers without the requisite purchasing power could gradually gain promotion by a slow process of advancing seniority. Commissions could also be bought from retiring officers and from those produced by death of an incumbent. These were filled by the promotion of the next available senior officer, which in turn created vacancies further down the list and so on. As indicated above, the lowest ranks could cost a considerable amount compared to the annual pay but the senior rank of Lt-Col was far more expensive: from

£4,500 (£308,674) for an infantry regiment up to £9,000 (£617,348) for the Foot Guards. Most would agree that this is a prohibitive sum of money that the majority of people would not have at hand today let alone then. Since the army had no pension scheme for officers, the purchase of commissions was a long-term investment and the higher the rank the higher the price that went with it.

The purchase system was superbly self-serving and self-perpetuating. It neatly fitted the requirements of the army which was a pure reflection of the larger rigid class structure that underpinned Victorian Britain. The sons of the rich joined from a sense of adventure or patriotism and sometimes the purchase of a commission set the seal on a family's social ascent. In other cases, a family with too many boys and too few opportunities bought a commission for a younger son to give him some sort of gainful employment. Strangely this last reason was similar to the motivations of most of the ordinary soldiers who joined to escape problems and lack of opportunities at home. Obviously, service in the colonies as an officer was a great opportunity for both social and political advancement upon returning home.

There were several consequences of this procedure until the late-19th century army reforms were carried out. The overall result was that it encouraged and favoured the privileged and the lazy and consequently de-motivated many of those who were as able or even more able but did not have an acceptable background or could not speak in the required fashion. This lack of open access had already been proven to be disastrous in the Crimea and even after the reforms were enacted the traditional attitudes lingered on right up to the First War. In short, it maintained a culturally and socially exclusive officer class drawn from the richest strata with private means and therefore a degree of financial independence.

Many of those involved regarded this as a positive rather than negative effect because, by buying their commission, officers

5. A 19th Century Officer

were subject only to army regulations and it was a clever way to ensure that the army remained independent of political control. This prevailing attitude and custom prevented the British Army from being embroiled in possible revolutionary activity or an outright coup d'état, unlike its French equivalent. Picture 5 shows a 19th Century Army Officer.

Emerging Classes

What about opportunities for the middle and trade classes as officers in the army? As the century progressed and the emerging commercial classes became increasingly wealthy their sons could also gain commissions as officers because their increased prosperity put the price of them within their reach. However, there was still the significant cultural and social barrier to overcome which meant that the financial requirement was not the only consideration. It was just not an attractive proposition socially because they were still not regarded as 'pukka' officers by the old upper class members. Consequently, this exclusive social climate discouraged many eminently qualified men from these middle social strata from choosing the army as a career. Needless to say, by the same token, this applied even more drastically to anyone from a working class or poor background.

The same pattern was replicated within the army structure itself. Experienced and competent serving Non Commissioned Officers (NCOs) could also gain commissions but the same class barrier applied to them even more rigidly. Apart from the basic purchase of the rank there was the additional expense of providing for one's own officer's uniform, cases and trunks for overseas postings, furniture, the batman's gear and a considerable amount of money to cover field sports and the all important social events.

There are always minority exceptions to all practices and in this context of commissions these were the 'gentlemen volunteers'. These were men hoping to gain a free commission by waiting for a vacancy in the organisation whilst serving as private soldiers but messing with the officers. The support of an influential politician or senior officer was also an important factor for these hopefuls.

Whether we now regard this purchase system and its effects as positive, or negative, obviously reflects an ideological position regarding the benefits of tradition as against progress. The fact is that even after the reforms brought about by the Crimean disaster and the abolition of the purchase system it was a very long time before the upper class stranglehold on commissions was broken. Tightly held tradition was still outweighing progress.

Ironically, by 1915, when the cream of the upper class officers had been virtually wiped out whilst showing the expected bravado required by their traditional training but in the inappropriate conditions, the middle classes were quickly called upon to make up the numbers. Nevertheless, a glance at any military history of that war shows that even then, when the army was technically more open to other classes becoming officers, the double barrelled names of the most senior commanders revealed the strength and duration of that legacy.

Disaster in the Crimea

Nowhere was this lack of upper class military ability more appositely demonstrated than during the Crimean War with Russia (1853-6) as outlined in a series of hard-hitting articles by *The Times* correspondent William Russell.[1] It was nearly forty years since we had defeated Napoleon at Waterloo, our last European war, but the largely aged generals who had fought in that war confidently thought that the army that was good enough to defeat him was more than good enough to beat the Russians. Therefore we committed to the Crimean campaign with our allies, France and Turkey, convinced it would be little more than a formality against an enemy that was now a shadow of its former self with its poor and demoralised people suffering under an autocratic regime and with a disorganised army.

As ever in British military history, and ironically as a startling foretaste of the Gallipoli disaster, it seems we considerably overestimated our own military prowess and organisation and woefully underestimated the will and resistance of the enemy. There is a tendency to fight the next war by the tactics of the last one and the British performance was a very apt application of it. The woefully crass decisions and approach by the highest ranking officers in the Crimea eventually spelled the death knell for the somewhat cosy élite purchasing arrangement. Not only that, but unlike our continental neighbours, our army was so small that practically the whole of it, between 30,000 and 50,000 (sources differ) was sent to fight in the Crimea and this left the home country bare of any real defenders.

As it turned out the war was not dispatched with the speed and ease that was confidently expected. Given the overall result and using a contemporary sporting comparison, the allies only won on a technicality although a 'score draw' would be a more accurate description.

The conduct of the administration, supply services and the army in that campaign was utterly appalling. This also applied to the medical support services at the old Turkish barracks hospital at Scutari. Surgeons were badly understaffed and yet initially turned down the help of Florence Nightingale's team of nurses. Generally speaking, at that time, nurses were drawn mainly from the poorer ranks of society and were little more than cleaners and cooks, even being looked down upon by batmen and servants. There were also many incidents of their drunken and promiscuous behaviour that resulted in some being sent home. Notwithstanding that, the Nightingale party worked hard to reduce the multifarious infections by introducing a strict hygiene and sanitation regime but was fighting a losing battle against what was later discovered to be an old open sewer running underneath the building.

Of course Florence Nightingale came from an upper class family matching the army officers and had many connections in high places so was well represented to the public back home. Mary Seacole, another nurse from a humbler background, offered her expertise and direct experience in the treatment of cholera to the Minister of War but was rejected by both him and Nightingale, suffering from a double prejudice because she was of mixed race. So she travelled to the war zone independently and despite being overshadowed back at home by her more famous contemporary, did equally as much separately to alleviate the suffering of the wounded soldiers. William Russell helped her gain much deserved later public recognition.

This verdict of maladministration and military incompetence particularly applies to the headquarters staff and commanding officers. One has only to think of the confusion and disorganisation that led to the misguided and futile charge of the Light Brigade into a massive barrage of Russian guns at Balaclava, as immortalised in the public consciousness by Alfred Tennyson's poem,[2] to see the need for a really radical change. Lord Cardigan, who led that charge, spent his nights not in the camp but aboard his luxury steam yacht and only joined his troops when he had breakfasted. Not only that but our main ally France had performed much better and this sounded alarm bells in the government. Something just had to be done about what became known widely as "Britain in Blunderland".[3]

Part-time Amateurs

Apart from the problems produced by the self-perpetuating officer class system, another tradition also dating from feudal origins, hampered any possible professionalism and central control in the preparedness of the army to meet the demands of modern warfare. This tradition was that armed forces were only raised as and when needed in wartime either as protection against invasion or as part of the King's levies abroad. In peacetime, county-based militias retained a small proportion of part-time local yeomen who were nominally trained in return for board and work and liable for call-up when home defence was needed. By being widely dispersed throughout the country-side these small local forces posed less of a threat to the general population and, indeed, these militias were regarded by the population as a safeguard of necessary liberties against despotic kings and other central controls.

The absolutist tendencies of both sides in the English Civil War, particularly the experience of "Oliver's Army"[4] further intensified the deeply felt traditional English fear and hatred of 'militarism'. There was a strong long standing aversion to any form of army permanently garrisoned at home. This was based on a justifiable fear that such an army could be easily hijacked by a tyrant to overthrow the civil government in a coup d'état in a time of crisis and destroy hard-won democracy and political liberty. Given those recent experiences, it is not at all surprising that the population would now only tolerate a small ad-hoc home reserve against possible invasion. In fact, in 1689, the Bill of Rights deemed the raising or keeping of a standing army in peacetime illegal without explicit Parliamentary consent. Near to home, the French Revolution and rise of Napoleon Bonaparte amply demonstrated the wisdom of this policy as did the military despotism in Spain and Austria during the remainder of the 19th century.

However, the newly formed Union of England and Scotland into Great Britain, in 1707, produced a contradictory need for a regular army particularly to fight the French and Dutch in Europe and help to establish and defend our new colonial empire in India and North America. Thus, in the early days of empire building a permanent and professional army was allowable as long as it met certain requirements: it remained voluntary and small, was recruited for a specific purpose and remained mainly well away from home, a bit of an oddity in military terms.

Despite the obvious imperative to adapt to changing conditions on the ground in Europe, this dispersal practice continued throughout the development of our colonial expansion with regular soldiers permanently posted at garrisons spread far and wide. Many new recruits were posted abroad almost immediately after finishing their basic training and my grandad Frank was one, being initially posted to South Africa for the Boer War and then to India and Burma. Apart from this obvious need to protect our economic interests abroad this was also a sort of disguised policy of convenience to avoid arousing that aforementioned suspicion of any hint of a significantly large standing home army. Britain preferred to cultivate her burgeoning naval power and command of the seas instead to protect its trade routes between home and the colonies.

Therefore, in the proper sense of the word, the British Army was not really an army at all with a large professional field force organised into segments under a single chain of command. It was scattered across the globe and engaged more in the role of a surrogate police force than a proper army, fighting small-scale and intermittent colonial expeditions to put down local native insurrections. The false impression of our army created by the media recounting of various heroics and exotic bravado against largely unorganised native foes in our empire had a *Boy's Own Paper* feel to it.[5]

This was a dangerous misapprehension which led to a smug belief that our army was a capable force that could handle any war that arose. Such as it was, it was populated by officers commissioned on ascribed socioeconomic status instead of military achievement. At the turn of the twentieth century, the result of this was a moribund and outmoded organisation that had not faced a fully trained and well armed European army for over eighty years.

Reform

After the disaster in the Crimea, a radical reform of the army was desperately needed and was urgently recommended, starting with a Royal Commission two years after that war, in 1858, which reported to Parliament in 1862. Although these reforms were mooted in the late 1850s it actually took another 10 years in a typically British fashion for them to be addressed properly by any kind of concerted action on the part of the government.

By this time, in addition to the memory of the woeful performance of the military in the Crimea, the dangerous expansionist rise of militaristic Prussia drove a worried Britain into thinking about creating a permanent standing home army and also a tenable reserve to protect us from invasion and to cover for those troops posted elsewhere. Prussia had established conscription in the previous century and its modern military expertise in the late 19th century was amply shown in the snap victory over a dilapidated Austria-Hungary in the 1866 seven-week war and then, not long after, in the unification of the disparate states and principalities of the loosely organised German Confederation into a powerful German Empire, after the defeat of France in 1871. This victory suddenly presented a real threat to our much treasured 'balance of power' strategy in Europe and increased the possibility of invasion in the future.

In fact, Royal Engineer Captain George Chesney's widely read pamphlet, 'The Battle of Dorking'[6] published in the same year, describes the fictitious invasion of southern England by a coincidentally German speaking foe! This was the author's allegorical way of alerting the public to the ramshackle state of the British Army and it far exceeded his expectations. It fired the public imagination and caused widespread panic and started an invasion phobia that permeated literature right through the First World War. John Buchan's 1915 story 'Thirty Nine Steps' is a case in point.

So the government eventually introduced a series of far-reaching reforms under the auspices of an ex-soldier, Edward Cardwell, Gladstone's Secretary of War, by a number of Acts in 1870 and 1871. Obstacles were immediate. Implementation was difficult and slow. The old 'die-hard' élite officer class led by the Duke of Cambridge, then Commander-in-Chief (C-in-C) and Queen Victoria's cousin, opposed any reform on principle. They wanted to maintain their grip on the army and preserve the proven tradition of the Dukes of York and Wellington that had culminated in victory at Waterloo. There was no going back though and the long overdue reforms were enacted.

From the beginning of the 19th century, the length of service for recruits had been 21 years, virtually a life sentence, and in harsh conditions that were like penal servitude. Flogging (abolished in 1868 but only in peacetime) was prevalent and occasional branding (only finally banned in 1871) was permitted for certain offences. An obvious lack of sufficient numbers, willing to take on such a 'life sentence' had led to it being reduced to 12 years, still considered too long by most. After finishing their first term soldiers were given a choice: be discharged or sign for another 12 year 'sentence'.

Those who went for the discharge option got nothing whereas those re-enlisting would receive a bounty and were promised a pension on completion. Interestingly, 20% of those electing to be discharged re-enlisted within 6 months. Obviously, for the majority of those from the lower class and the poor, with little or no work opportunities and therefore not having much alternative experience, professional soldiering with its secure accommodation, regular meals and a wage was a big motivation for many but not all.

Cardwell introduced 'short service': enlistment was now officially for 12 years but in actuality was for six years in the front line regulars, the remaining time being spent in a nominally paid reserve, liable for brief annual training and active recall.

Regimental districts (counties and densely populated areas) were created and men previously posted willy-nilly to general service could choose which regiment to be posted to after a period of initial training. This reinforced the principle of an army of locals whereby soldiers were serving with peers from their own area or even their own street. Regimental battalions were reformed and a rotation system initiated, so that the 1st Battalion would serve overseas whilst the 2nd Battalion would remain at the home base and vice versa. Also, in 1871, 26,000 troops were recalled from the self-governing colonies which were now required to produce their own militias.

It was the traditionally accepted practice of purchasing military commissions which was the really contentious aspect of the army's structure though. This had been ritually abused by army commanders and, as we saw in some high profile cases, their spouses as well and had been sanctioned well into the Victorian era by Wellington. Much to the chagrin of the old guard, this was finally abolished. Along with this decision, the ad-hoc dispersed army was finally organised on a permanent professional basis although it remained much smaller than its European counterparts. This led Kaiser William to refer to the British Expeditionary Force to France (BEF), holding up the German advance in 1914, as a "contemptible little army", an epithet enthusiastically adopted by the men who then began calling themselves 'The Old Contemptibles' with pride!

Ironically given further blunders by commanders at Gallipoli and The Somme, this army eventually became the efficient technological fighting force that finally beat the Kaiser's Germans on the Western Front in 1918.

The Ordinary Soldier

What about the backgrounds of the ordinary soldiers? In the 1850s, 20% of ordinary soldiers were totally illiterate and only a small percentage barely literate. This is no surprise given the almost complete lack of available education for the vast majority of the population. Schooling was inextricably linked to class background and so the majority of recruits, from the lower reaches of this structurally rigid society, would have received at best the most basic education, if any at all. Until the Education Act of 1870, education was largely a private affair, and apart from the upper class independent schools and middle class grammar schools, the vast majority of the population made the best of what local teaching was on offer. Mostly, this was a hit and miss affair disparately provided by some philanthropic or religious individuals or groups.

In 1846, for instance, an experienced recruiting sergeant remarked that two thirds of all recruits joined because otherwise they faced nothing but destitution. The rest were the unskilled working class, although still called by the derogatory term 'lower classes'. The 1870 Act laid the foundations of an improved civilian education system which, in turn, gradually translated into the army. Between 1874 and 1880, 61% soldiers were culled from unskilled casual workers, such as farm workers, servants or factory fodder.

The majority of this poor sector, faced with very limited job opportunities, signed up out of desperation: to quit humdrum or arduous jobs, to escape from family, local area problems or, probably the single most overarching factor, likely unemployment and poverty. Another important motivation was that upon enlisting a man would be excused all debts up to £30.

At that time, along with bricklayers, farm labourers earned about 15 old shillings/75p a week (now £51.45p), worked throughout daylight hours, mostly lived in tied cottages which usually had no water, at least maybe cold but certainly not hot, and no electricity. Rent was on average about 3 shillings/15p a week (now £10.30p) and stout boots cost at least a week's wages, a huge chunk of one's earnings.

Even though the pay was only a shilling/5p a day compared with some jobs at four shillings/20p a day, the army provided the possibility of a secure lifelong career and, most important, regular square meals and free accommodation. Being in uniform was a big catch. It provided the soldier with the opportunity of impressing girls back in the village or nearby town and showing everyone that he had amounted to something in life. Not only that, but after basic training, the recruit and mates from his own locality would most likely be posted abroad with his local regiment in places far more exotic than their home towns in rural or industrial Britain.

Frank and two of his brothers joined up because they were born and lived in a tiny village deep in the Essex countryside with a very limited choice of work on the land and sought to escape this and expand their horizons. Interestingly, recruiting staffs observed that those from rural backgrounds were more robust and much fitter than those from the urban slums, not very surprising when you think about it.

These motives mirror those of today's young men from depressed urban backgrounds. In the 1860s, The General Army Inspectorate observed that: "Recruits joining the army belong to a considerable extent to the lower classes" and that: "Many are men whose character would not bear inspection." So by contemporary sociological standards they would be regarded at best as the rough end of the working class and at worst a criminal underclass. By 1901, the year my grandfather joined, according to Richard Holmes (2002): "Well over 90% had no jobs in the civilian world."

As to ordinary soldiers becoming officers this presented a substantial barrier. Even up to the turn of the century, 30 years after purchasing was abolished, commissions from the ranks were still rare. Those wishing to be officers still required a combination of intangible social position accompanied by a large financial reserve to meet the extra expense of the lifestyle. This expectation was well illustrated by the heroes of Rorke's Drift in 1879 when some NCOs and Privates who were offered commissions declined because they did not fit in or could not afford to take them.

Other ranks could theoretically gain officer promotion but few of them went beyond RSM/Warrant Officer Class 1 (WO1), the highest non-commissioned rank. Anyone proceeding beyond that point was rewarded for being brave in the field or talented. Also, any existing NCO making it beyond a Captain's rank was still unusual and reaching beyond that to a higher field rank was indeed a rarity.

However, Frank along with many NCOs followed one well-trodden route through this difficult terrain which was to become a regiment's Quartermaster (QM). This could often eventually lead to an accompanying Lieutenant's rank. Against this historical and social background, Frank, from very humble rural beginnings was commissioned as Lt after 22 years service and this was a reward for his ability, service and field experience in many campaigns. As he never had any real money and was continually moving around in rented army accommodation in different postings, mainly abroad, it was certainly not his class or monetary background that did it for him. Finally, his achievement of the rank of Major before retirement was sociologically noteworthy even then, given the traditional structure of the army and the social and financial restrictions of society.

Training

At that time, basic training was about eight weeks and upon finishing there was allocation to, or choice of specialist training. On completing his training, Frank attended a Mounted Infantry (MI) course before being posted abroad to South Africa to immediately apply this training in combat. The usual practice for new recruits was to send them to a Regimental depot, where they received basic marching and disciplinary training usually about four times a day for about three months.

Identifying exactly what training methods were adopted is difficult and many commentators say it was because it mainly comprised boring and repetitive parade ground drilling. This endless drilling, known by soldiers' slang as 'square bashing', was paramount and instilled the instinctive obedience to any command however strange. This was obviously crucial in the chaos of a battlefield situation where discipline and ordered formation could make the difference between surviving and being killed. The recruits were then sent off to a main training camp where they learned tactics. Not unusually, the first three months were in England, and further training was then conduced at their first posting wherever that was.

This ingrained discipline carried over into civilian life when the soldier was off duty and in 'mufti'. It was regularly observed that one could tell a soldier or retired soldier in civvies at a passing glance because of his military bearing which replicated the barrack square marching, shoulders back and an upright stance and purposeful gait at all times.

1899-1902

The early part of the Boer War demonstrated yet again, that despite the stated intention to learn from the Crimean experience, how out of touch our army remained in its tactical manoeuvres. In short, the well-honed tradition of British set-pieces was no match for the Boer farmers who adopted guerrilla tactics like the American Colonials in the War of Independence. This meant that sheer force of numbers counted for very little against a mobile enemy hidden in the ground cover with devastating long-range rifle power.

It was a big shock to an army used to easily quelling previous colonial uprisings in Africa. However, after the initial shock it slowly began to adapt to the prevailing flexible tactics. One innovation was the introduction of the MI units for which Frank was trained and these were able to reach the enemy at speed and drive them into the open.

Like the Crimea, the Boer War was a pyrrhic victory with the Army of Victoria being severely tested and found wanting in its thinking and tactics. This time, the intention to change needed to be accompanied by serious and prompt action to back up the words. Between the end of the Boer War in 1902 and the start of the Great War, the army started a gradual transformation from what was really a colonial police force into a modern European army equipped with the effective Lee Enfield rifle, machine guns and heavy artillery.

1914-18

By 1914, many observers believed that, although it was much smaller than other comparable European armies, it was the best in the world being an army of highly trained professionals with many NCOs who had recent conflict experience. The campaigns in Gallipoli and The Somme once again gave the lie to this view.

As training got more advanced, sometimes a battlefield was marked out in the countryside and a mock battle took place and this simulation approach gradually became more important, especially leading up to WW1. During that war, new techniques were taught on a regular basis, and eventually working with tanks and learning flexible storm-troop type tactics were a must. Men in the artillery were taught modern techniques for better accuracy.

In 1914, the vast surge of eager volunteers responding to Earl Kitchener's appeal completely overwhelmed available supplies. Many had to use their own clothes, others ended up in out of date uniforms whilst yet others wore emergency uniforms, the so-called "Kitchener Blues" a reference to both the Earl and the colour. This was to be repeated in 1940 with the Local Volunteer Force soon popularly known as the Home Guard.

At the outbreak of war the army was still largely characterised by a personalised command structure operating through patronage and a protégé system. There was a small and élite band of 15,000 officers and of those, over 50% were the sons of army officers, a continuation of the neat cultural and social transmission discussed. Most of these sons of the rich had enlisted to avoid the ignominy of going into 'trade' as paid employment was considered unsuitable and to be avoided at all costs, except in the church or army. Ironically, many of their fathers had originally made their large fortunes in the self same despised sphere.

Despite the advantages of social background and all that went with it, the officers in this reformed army were now expected to gain promotion by actual demonstration of their abilities. This had occurred before but only in a minority of cases. The army had now finally arrived at an emerging and more encompassing meritocracy that allowed some patronage on entry but then relied on duty and performance in the field for due reward.

Enter the Great War playing its dreadful part in changing the shape of the British Army. As the war progressed on its bloody path the death toll mounted alarmingly as a consequence of the attritional trench warfare produced by industrial weaponry. More men were desperately needed to plug a gaping hole. Most original officers who had started out at the front died there between 1914 and 1915. Conscription in 1916 replenished the losses and 235,000 more men were commissioned although most were temporary elevations. This finally broke the back of the élite system and large numbers of ordinary people got in on the commission act by default as the army had to rapidly reinvent itself to face increasingly threatening demands of the changing nature of warfare.

Like all other institutions the army directly reflected its society and its time. This general chapter is included in my grandfather's individual story, not to knock the class basis of the British Army, but rather to show its journey in period of great transition as a background to his remarkable advance through its ranks.

NOTES

1. Dr. William Charles Russell, graduate of Trinity College, Dublin, was an Irishman who wrote for *The Times*. During the Crimean War he was that newspaper's Special Correspondent for two years and his hard hitting reports from the front deeply shocked the readers and led to demands for change. He was also responsible for bringing the work of Mary Seacole to the wider public.

2. Alfred Lord Tennyson was Poet Laureate from 1850 to 1892. His famous poem, "The Charge of the Light Brigade" is a tribute to the brave men who lost their lives at Balaclava owing to miscommunication between the commanders. This verse, known to most students of English Literature, captures the gist:

> "Cannon to right of them,
> Cannon to left of them,
> Cannon in front of them
> Volley'd and thunder'd;
> Storm'd at with shot and shell,
> Boldly they rode and well,
> Into the jaws of Death,
> Into the mouth of Hell
> Rode the six hundred."

3. "Britain in Blunderland" was a phrase quickly adopted on the publication of Lewis Carroll's "Alice in Wonderland" in 1865 as a label to describe the recent events in the Crimea War

4. "Oliver's Army" is a song written by Elvis Costello after a visit to Belfast in 1978. The title alludes to Oliver Cromwell's Model Army in the Civil War linking it to the modern British Army.

5. The Boy's Own Paper (1879-1967) was a magazine of gripping adventure stories, puzzles and various competitions aimed at teenage boys. There were many famous contributors, such as: Robert Baden-Powell (founder of the Boy Scout Movement), Arthur Conan Doyle, WG Grace, Rudyard Kipling and Jules Verne. The phrase 'Boy's Own' is used nowadays to describe daring or improbable feats of heroism that formed the content of the paper. In the late-19th century it was associated with the empire and a jingoistic attitude.

6. In May 1871, Captain George Chesney contributed this short story to 'Blackwood Magazine'. Despite being ostensibly fictitious he wanted to alert everyone to the swift and unexpected Prussian victory in the recent Franco-Prussian War 1870-71, resulting in the creation of a new German Empire and a future foe.

It certainly achieved his aim, greatly alarming the public by drawing attention to the lack of preparedness of the nation and its army fuelled by an arrogant belief in the natural superiority of the British and their culture over other powers. It was later republished in many editions and translations and is considered a founding piece of the "invasion literature" genre.

4.

Frank's War and Peace

FRANK BAILEY began his army career when enlisting at the beginning of the twentieth century and being posted as an ordinary soldier to South Africa. After the Boer War he saw colonial service in India, Burma and Mauritius and was then directly involved as an NCO in the major campaigns of the Great War.

Frank was born in Copford, a tiny village in Essex near Colchester into a farmer's family in the late 19th century. Even today the old part of what is still a village retains an exceptionally rural environment. The population in the 1901 Census was recorded as 684 and was not much over 1,000 ninety years later.

In those first years of the 20th century, there was no running water in the village so it had to be drawn from wells, only a few of which had pumps and there was no electricity or street lighting. The village was made up from a few scattered cottages and farms. Life on a farm in late Victorian England was tough and whilst there was some rudimentary mechanisation, most labour was mainly by hand and lasted throughout daylight hours. Employment was extremely limited especially since the great depression of the previous thirty years which had severely truncated the agricultural sector. The only regular job was on the farm his father worked or elsewhere on the land for someone else. For Frank, seeking adventure, the choice was obvious.

The pattern was already set by his older siblings of whom two, Joseph and Elizabeth, had emigrated to America and others who were married and living elsewhere. Frank did not see any real point in stopping in a village with no real work opportunities or social life and thought his chances of individual success and reward lay elsewhere. Like many other village boys he went to the city. The nearest sizeable town then was Colchester, about 5 miles away, but Frank was thinking much bigger than that.

London was in his sights and so he caught the train and moved to the capital in search of his fortune. He got a job as a barman but this soon palled. An even larger and exotic world of the colonies now beckoned so he joined the regular army on 12th March 1901. From that moment his destiny was to change forever. After completing the basic training in July of that year, he was posted to the 1st Battalion, Essex Regiment in which he spent the majority of his army career.

Still on the excitement trail he signed up for the specially formed Mounted Infantry Company. These units were initiated for South Africa to combat the mobility of the Boers in their guerrilla war and take them on at their own game. They were not cavalry in the usual sense but infantry soldiers trained to ride fast and surprise the Boers in the scrubland striking quickly by firing from their mounts before the enemy could reposition its machine guns.

This detachment appealed to the brighter segment of recruits who were highly self-motivated and would thrive on the challenges of the army life if they stayed on after their short service time was completed. They were specifically instructed in horse care, riding skills, map reading, scouting, reporting and self reliance.

Boer War: 1901-2

He served his country there as a member of the MI during the latter stages of the Boer War between November 1901 and October 1902. In his first year of active service he was almost immediately appointed Lance Corporal, an honorary position not a promoted rank, because of the urgent need for competent troop leaders. In times of conflict, men gained the lower NCO ranks early on as a result of distinguished service in the field. Frank was now on the first rung of a ladder that would eventually stretch to greater heights over the coming years. No details are available of his individual activities in South Africa but given his later exploits in the Great War it is most likely that he was singled out for early promotion as a result of his wholehearted involvement in the battalion's objectives.

Frank is photographed in uniform as a Lance-Corporal (L-Cpl) at a studio in Warley which was the headquarters base of the Essex Regiment (Picture 6, next page). With the breeches and spurs this is the MI uniform. Frank passed his MI course at Aldershot in 1901 so this puts this photo at around 1902-03 on his return from the Boer War.

6. Lance Corporal Frank Bailey in Mounted Infantry Uniform

Before Frank arrived in South Africa, 1st Essex had already shown bravery by featuring notably in successful actions: the Relief of Kimberley, the Battle at Paardeberg, taking the surrender of Cronje and his 4,000 men and the Driefontein engagement where they engaged in a surprisingly spontaneous and successful bayonet charge (Burrows 1931). He arrived after those distinguished engagements were over but was later directly involved in the guarding of the 'blockhouse' lines.

In June 1902, as a specially appointed Honorary Corporal for the occasion, Frank along with eleven other men was selected to represent the Essex Regiment at the coronation of Edward VII. However, the King needed an urgent appendix operation so the ceremony was delayed. He and his regimental colleagues left South Africa for the coronation in August 1902 but he did not return to Warley until October so it is likely they returned to South Africa in the interim. By this time the Boer war was over and the 1st Battalion had left for India in September, travelling via the Seychelles and Colombo in Ceylon (Sri Lanka). However, there is a bit of a mystery here because he was not posted with them.

Oddly, although a Battalion NCO, instead of accompanying his battalion Frank stayed home at Warley Barracks, the Regiment Headquarters (HQ) on returning from South Africa. He became an Acting Corporal (Cpl) on 17th October but on L-Cpl's pay. He followed them to India six months later.

He was posted in the 2nd Battalion from 24th July until posted back to 1st Battalion in India on 6th March 1903. The explanation is that this was a common practice following a promotion for the man to change units as the army wanted only men of equal rank to mix and drink together as a matter of maintaining discipline. As we saw in the previous chapter the 1st Bn would be abroad when the 2nd was at home base.

Colonial Travels

For the next five years Frank was mainly based in India supporting the Indian Army. Although an NCO, with battle experience from South Africa, yet again he did not accompany a limited detachment of the battalion to the Somaliland Protectorate to combat the Dervish forces of Mohammed Abdullah Hassan, dubbed the Mad Mullah by the British. This was because he was involved in both supervising the training of recent recruits and enhancing his own educational career.

During his time in India he was eventually promoted to Corporal in 1906, having passed his exams two years before and a vacancy occurring. He was stationed at Bangalore and engaged in transport duties for which he gained a certificate in July followed fairly quickly by promotion to Lance-Sergeant. Frank was moving up the through the ranks yet again. He was enjoying his time in the army abroad, thousands of miles from the limited horizon of his village at home in Essex so, at about the same time he also signed up to extend his service to *"complete 12 years with the colors"*, with army clerical spelling error. This now showed a real commitment to becoming a regular professional soldier which meant that he would now serve until at least 1913. Initially, he had enlisted under the post-Boer War 'Short Service' regulations, which was for an initial term of 3 years but this had been extended for another 3 years until 1907.

The battalion was now transferred to Burma, then part of India, from December 1906 but Frank spent a period *"invalided home in March 1907"* (*Essex Regiment Gazette*, ERG). Without details one assumes it was some debilitating disease contracted whilst there. As to the Burmese expedition, this was yet another British action to monitor and combat the Young Men's Buddhist Association, a copy of and rival to the YMCA which was linked to the rise of aggressive nationalism. Not for the first time they were deployed as peacekeeping policemen in the event of any rebellion.

Then it was off to Ireland between 1908 and 1909 at the Curragh Camp, County Kildare, South West of Dublin with A Company 2nd Battalion.

The men of 2nd Battalion had been in Dublin in April 1907, long before he was posted and were mainly stationed between the Curragh and Wellington Barracks in Dublin.

Whilst at the Curragh he was engaged in supervising training exercises and manoeuvres but also had time to meet and date his future wife Rosanne Howe, who hailed from Kildare. This was a common occurrence as many British soldiers met the local women both on duty as part of their tasks and also off duty at various social events laid on in the community. The duration of his stay with the 2nd Battalion Irish posting is unclear because the ERG says he volunteered: *"for foreign service again in 1908"* whereas Army records have him dispatched to India in November 1909 for another four years. There was clearly a gap between him volunteering in Ireland and then eventually actually being posted on Foreign Service.

Apart from the half battalion posted to address the problems of the rebellious Mullah in Somaliland and the Burmese expedition to control the Young Buddhists, the period from 1904 up to 1913 was a relatively quiet period of colonial service during which time the battalion engaged in training exercises and many sporting and army related competitions. Uncharacteristically, in his 1st Battalion book, John Burrows glosses over this period. During this time grandad Frank became the best rifle shot in his company and excelled at a number of sporting pursuits whilst at Quetta, in Baluchistan (then India). He was clearly developing into an army all rounder.

Behind all the apparent calm there was a very different picture in the background. The battalion was also regularly involved in engagements on the North West Frontier Province of India. This was created as a separate entity in 1901 by artificially dividing the tribal territories and governing indirectly through the diverse leaders to avoid the previous conflicts that had cost many thousands of British soldiers' lives. This was an exemplar of the old adage 'divide and rule'.

This derelict mountainous part of the region, including the notorious Khyber Pass, formed the vital passage between India and Afghanistan. This whole border area required a large trained regular force tied down in a constant state of readiness to defend it from the local tribesmen and their internecine conflicts. There were sporadic but regular attacks on the army detachments not to mention a well-developed gun running business. More importantly there was always the looming presence of the Russian bear lurking around the mountains threatening to infiltrate this northern boundary and take a big bite out of this vitally strategic corner of the British Empire.

As a result, the men of Essex were posted for a routine tour of duty as part of the large standing 'Army of India' which combined the British Army in India, a rotating Colonial Force with units from Britain along with the 'Indian army', recruited from the local population and with expatriate British officers. Postings in the latter service were less prestigious but better paid although the officers were expected to have a grasp of basic Hindi as most of the men were from those areas.

Colloquially this tour of duty was known by the men as the "*frontier or mountain*" warfare. Frank was periodically posted in both armies, a common occurrence for NCOs as they were needed for the training of both sets of troops. Because of the prevailing conditions the army decided it had to adapt and adopt a new approach to combat the highly mobile tribesmen and, learning from their experiences in South Africa, reorganised themselves into small highly trained and lightly equip-ped units which proved to be very successful. Frank's South African MI experience came in handy for his training role.

Whilst in that part of the country, wearing the Queen's South Africa Medal, he married Rosanne Howe in Karachi on 9th October 1910 in Full Dress Tunic (Picture

7. *Sergeant Frank marries Rosanne in India*

7). By all accounts Rosanne was a strikingly attractive woman with a big shock of auburn hair. Being a married on foreign duty was a smart move for a soldier as a wife was able to expand his social experience considerably in the constant colonial whirl of parties, dinners and sporting occasions, now called social networking.

In 1911, Frank became the Orderly Room Corporal, an appointment in the Regimental Administrative Office which rewarded men who showed ability in applying the army's systems. This was a significant year for him. On 15th June Frank and Rose had a son, Frederick William Charles, in Quetta. He was my father. Apart from parenthood, the years 1912 and 1913 were relatively routine years and as he was very settled he took a further opportunity to update his education being awarded two 1st Class Certificates in March and September 1912. Early in the following year Frank gained the next rank of progress as Orderly Room Sergeant at Battalion HQ. Now as a Sergeant (Sgt) and having decided that the army life was definitely the ticket for him, he reengaged with 1st Battalion in Quetta to complete 21 years service which was the usual maximum period.

Shortly after this, in November 1913, Sergeant Frank with the HQ staff and half of the battalion, comprising nine officers and 396 other ranks, left Karachi for Mauritius as part of an Indo-Colonial Relief Force. Frank was stationed on this beautiful island for 12 days as part of his Indian service and then for one year as British. The other half of the battalion went to Durban. This was the situation until December 1914. In August 1914, war had broken out in Europe and the two halves of the 1st Battalion were recalled home to Warley Barracks. Frank and Ernest were now ready for their part in the Great War.

Great War: 1914-18

Like most of his generation Frank was actively involved in most of the major battles of the war but survived them all. What chance did he have of surviving one battle yet alone all? He left Gallipoli in one piece which, given the short odds, was a stroke of fortune but to emerge unscathed from the dreadful first day at Beaumont Hamel in The Somme was extremely lucky when one considers the terrible carnage involved.

To carry on through 1917 at Arras in France, onto Ypres and Passchendaele in Flanders and then the famous tank battle at Cambrai, where he earned an award for gallantry in the field, was nothing short of amazing. It was the military equivalent of winning a vast accumulator bet.

1914

At the end of 1914, 1st Essex with Sgt Frank Bailey was included as part of the 88th Brigade of the newly formed 29th Division, with 4th Worcester, 2nd Hampshire and 5th Royal Scots. This division was mainly made up from regular troops recently returned from India. They were posted for intensive training in the Midlands.

1915

There was much discussion in the overall command structure as to whether the 29th Division should go to the Western Front or to the Middle East and the result was that they were posted to Egypt. Therefore a thousand men of the battalion went with the brigade to Avonmouth to catch a ship to Alexandria. The SS 'Caledonia' set sail with the Essex, assessed in glowing terms as they assembled by a Major Muir from the Royal Scots.

Now Frank was part of the Mediterranean Expeditionary Force (MEF) and on the voyage to Alexandria he supervised much training in formations for landing in the face of opposition, this activity being continued using rope ladders whilst in Alexandria Harbour. During this time the very recently appointed Commander-in-Chief (C-in-C), General Sir Ian Hamilton, inspected the division without 1st Essex who arrived the same day.

On 14th April, Frank's battalion sailed to Mudros, on the Greek island of Lemnos, in readiness for the planned assault at Cape Helles on the Gallipoli Peninsula. Ten days later, they set sail for Gallipoli to arrive on what was that fateful Sunday morning, 25th April and land on W Beach at about 10.00 hours. Brother Ernest was also there.

A more detailed account of that action is given under *Gallipoli*. It was a hellish Helles as the 1st Essex were initially squashed on a very narrow beach overlooked by bluffs from which the Turkish defenders could pick them off fairly easily. They eventually managed to get inland by nightfall.

It was a constant and fierce fighting situation without any real respite and their CO, Lt-Col Godfrey-Fawcett, was killed in action during a heavy Turkish attack on 2nd May trying to lead a counter attack. Two weeks after that, Frank was made up to Acting RSM in the field and Ernest was also promoted to Sergeant. Undoubtedly, in this dire theatre the army desperately needed men with fighting and organisational experience which both had gained in a variety of actions in the years before the war.

Frank was back in Alexandria later in that year where he was properly promoted to RSM/WO1 rejoining his battalion in September. In October Frank had a very near miss at Suvla Bay when the Adjutant, Major Wood, was shot in the neck by a sniper whilst leaning outside his dug out, smoking his pipe and having a quick look at a passing aeroplane. "*He took his pipe out of his mouth, made a gesture of annoyance, then sank back into the arms of the Sergeant Major with the words: 'I am finished, SM.'*" (Burrows: 199). That Sergeant Major was my grandad. Major Wood is commemorated at Ingatestone Church and is shown in Picture 54 with colleagues in 1914.

1916

In January, Frank helped to organise the battalion for the evacuation from the peninsula which ironically was far more successful then the landings. March saw him and 1st Essex in France reassigned to the British Expeditionary Force (BEF). He was given leave to the UK at the beginning of April and then returned to France for a course conducted at Flexicourt, near Abbeville on the River Somme, rejoining the battalion in the field on 23rd May. He was billeted at Louvencourt from 15th June, coincidentally my father's fifth birthday, as they were making ready for what was to be the notorious first day of the Somme.

Despite keeping busy with his RSM duties did Frank's thoughts roam to home? Thoughts of his young son on his birthday must have impinged poignantly on Frank's consciousness. From our contemporary standpoint we can never really know for sure what those men felt as they prepared for what was billed the Big One. What our common human experience tells us, is this: all the men, especially those who were fathers, could not totally divorce their familial feelings from what was happening here on the Western front.

His battalion was posted with the 1st Newfoundlanders at Beaumont Hamel in the northern sector of the Somme front, near Thiepval and the Ancre River, and took part in the first morning's attack on 1st July. This was the second time in succession that his battalion had been involved at the very outset of a campaign. It turned out to be a disastrous day for all concerned in that sector and one of the worst spots for devastating loss of men. A more detailed outline of that particular attack is included elsewhere in *The Somme*. During that first dreadful morning RSM Bailey was encouraging and organizing the men along the blocked communication trench before they went over the top. All those concerned that day were in the thick of the deadliest fighting of the front so far and Frank again emerged as one of the lucky ones.

After that he was extremely busy with both the combatant and the organisational side of his job as RSM, which involved planning mining attacks and repairing the defences although there was some time for a few sporting occasions to break up the routine. He was directly engaged in the battalion's successful taking of German trenches at Gueudecourt, in front of Bapaume. His company also featured in the capture of over 60 Brandenburgers.

Looking back, my grandfather Frank was a veteran NCO with conflict experience from South Africa and Gallipoli and his experiences on the 'hellish Helles' beaches over a year before held him in good stead in the heat of the battle for Beaumont Hamel. Nevertheless, having survived Gallipoli he was especially lucky to live through this latest dreadful bloodbath. Ironically, after this was over he unwittingly rode his luck away from the front by nearly getting shot by mistake. In December at Montagne, says Burrows, an officers' party was shooting at deer bolting across the landscape: "*when to their horror they noticed RSM Bailey's party in the line of fire in the valley. Luckily there were no casualties.*" Being shot for a deer would have been ignominious compared to being shot by the enemy in battle!

1917

This was the busiest year of the war for the battalion and the most significant one for Frank who fought with distinction throughout the campaign. Entered as: "*Bailey, RSM, F.*" he was mentioned by the C-in-C, Field Marshal Sir Douglas Haig in his dispatches: "*for distinguished and gallant services and devotion to duty*" at the Battle of Monchy-le-Preux in April. This citation is published in *The London Gazette* for 25th May.

The Monchy engagement was part of the larger Battle of Arras which had started on Easter Sunday and the 1st Essex were given a very hard time. With the battalion all but wiped out, RSM Frank helped Lt Lawson organise a desperate defence in the face of a severe German counterattack. The remainder of the battalion and HQ staff defended in the streets of Monchy with barricades. Despite the enemy onslaught the resistance of these men along with their peers 1st Newfoundland broke the advance of the élite Bavarian Division.

Later on, RSM Bailey was awarded the Serbian Cross of Karageorge, 1st Class, with Swords, as "*Conferred by the King of Serbia*" in *The London Gazette* of 23rd February. Lacking exact details, this highest Serbian award was most likely part of a quota of awards and decorations that the Allied Governments periodically doled out for sustained good service rather than gallant conduct. Each CO would be asked to nominate someone for service awards and Frank was chosen doubtless because of his long uninterrupted service at the front of the main campaigns, especially at Gallipoli.

Now Frank entered a dramatic period. On 7th August, he was admitted to 14th Corps Rest Station, Field Ambulance with "*myalgia*" a rheumatic or muscular condition requiring some rest. This was clearly an early sign of the increasing fatigue that the constant fighting and uninterrupted heavy physical exercise required by maintaining defences and training for attack was having on the frontline NCOs and troops. The wonder is that anyone remained 100% fit in these conditions. On rejoining the battalion later that month he was unaware that elder brother Edgar had just been registered as having died from wounds received around Ypres.

The 1st Essex with the Hampshire now engaged in an integrated attack with the artillery and the Royal Flying Corps (RFC) at dawn on 16th August near Langemarck in Flanders, north of Ypres. For a week they were subjected to continuous heavy shelling and Frank's company had to take shelter inside a half-made pillbox.

The drama of war intensified. On 26th September, his 35th birthday, Frank was gassed whilst at Langemarck but remained "*at duty*" despite this injury which strongly suggests that it was mercifully not as serious as to prevent him from staying at the front. Very often, if not so dangerous as to require specialist medical treatment, the men would bravely insist on staying just behind the field of action. This particularly occurred if they felt too much fuss would ensue from having to be withdrawn from the front, formally attend an ambulance station and be involved in what they considered far too much unnecessary paper work.

After Passchendaele, which raged through uncharacteristically heavy August rainfall and the notorious viscous mud forming a quagmire every bit as dangerous as the enemy, preparations were made for the action to take Cambrai. Gaining control of this town was vital as it was a strategic road and rail junction and also a jumping off point for any advance further on into Flanders.

Training for Cambrai was intensively conducted throughout September only being relieved by a Corps drumming competition which 1st Essex won under the auspices of Frank's brother Ernest, the Regimental Sergeant Drummer. Obviously not known at the time but Cambrai was to be the last battle that the 1st Battalion, as part of 88th Brigade would fight with the 29th Division.

This was the first battle where massed ranks of tanks were used which according to Liddell Hart (1970) was "One of the landmarks in the history of warfare, the dawn of a new epoch." The battalion was given the task of seizing the bridge at Masnières to aid the advance to the town of Cambrai. Frank's company was in the very front of the attack from the 'off' on the morning of 20th November but the attack stalled when a tank collapsed the bridge. They were subjected to sniper fire but after nightfall they successfully mopped them up and by 03.00 hours on the 21st the road was clear.

During the course of this battle Frank, as RSM was awarded the DCM, the equivalent of the officer's DSO (Distinguished Service Order) and at that time the highest NCO medal award known colloquially by the army as 'the near VC' for: "*conspicuous gallantry and devotion to duty. When battalion headquarters became involved in heavy sniping from housetops he ran the gauntlet for a hundred yards, trying to find a route by which to extricate them. When battalion headquarters became involved in an attack he ably assisted the commanding officer.*" (*The London Gazette,* 1918)

After his dangerous sprinting he was rewarded with being sent back to base for a posting to the home establishment leaving France on 23rd December, arriving at the Warley HQ for an "*exchange*" posting just in time for a Christmas in England.

1918

While at home Frank was variously attached to four other battalions throughout January and February undoubtedly for training purposes. Being an RSM with all his combat and service experience, he was prized as a trainer who could impart many vital battlefield and survival skills.

Frank was photographed (Picture 8) as RSM/WO1 after 25th April 1918, the third anniversary of Gallipoli. The date is known because on the lower right arm below the RSM rank badge are three chevrons, instituted in 1915 that indicate three years of overseas service (1915-18). At the top of the left arm is the red triangle of the 29th Division, widely acknowledged as the

"*Incomparable 29th*" of which the 1st Essex was a member. At the bottom the vertical stripe indicates a wound as sustained on active service in the field, in his case being gassed at Langemarke in Belgium.

The 29th Division was made up of a concentration of regular battalions taken from the Empire and mustered at home for the first day of Gallipoli. Their red triangle distinguished them as much respected soldiers wherever they went because of their fighting record. After Cambrai, there was a brigade reduction in the size of 29th Division on 1st February and as a result 1st Essex was transferred to 37th Division. This decision went

8. RSM/WO1 Frank Bailey, DCM

down very badly with all of them, including the GOCs and COs, and many continued to wear the red triangle long after as a badge of honour despite the new divisional insignia. It was very unlikely that anyone, including officers, would have dared to confront an experienced RSM about this. Although home at the time of the transfer, Frank had served consistently with the "*Incomparable 29th*" from Gallipoli right through to Cambrai being directly involved those battles for those three years.

As the senior NCO in the battalion he was always close to the CO and had a key position in HQ Staff. The Sergeant Major's position was that of the man in the middle, between the officers and the other ranks, 'the binding glue'. During peacetime this was an all purpose role of administrator, interpreter of orders and such tasks as supervising and training of the men under his command. In conflict he had to lead and be an example to the men, organising the supply of ammo, assisting the adjutant in whatever way possible, coordinating defence, also giving and maintaining confidence to new recruits.

On 30th September, Frank and Rose had a daughter Rose Enid Muriel, aka my aunt "Billy", born in Dedham, near Colchester, Essex. The Great War finally ground to a halt at 11.00 hours on 11th November 1918. Peace had finally arrived after four and a quarter years of the most horrendous conflict ever seen that had eliminated a whole generation of men in all the countries that had taken part.

In April 1919, the battalion of six officers and 780 other ranks, under Acting Major Paxton, whom Frank had ably assisted as RSM in the trenches at Beaumont Hamel on that dreadful day in 1916, left Belgium by train from Charleroi to Antwerp and onto Tilbury Dock. After much demobilisation administration, Frank finally arrived at Warley Barracks on 7th May, where as RSM and Regimental QM, he was posted to the Depot and also immediately assigned to 2nd Battalion, again as a trainer.

A month later, having been posted back to his old 1st Battalion, he participated in the Paris Victory Parade with five colleagues on Bastille Day, 14th July and then the equivalent parade in London three days later.

On 31st August he and the battalion arrived at Kinsale in Ireland. About 400 men had anticipated that they were to be demobilised post-war but by December only about 50 officers and other ranks were actually discharged. Early in 1920, the men were reorganized to incorporate the influx of many replacement recruits and to meet the demands of some unorthodox Irish Republican Army (IRA) activity in the South West.

Unfortunately many of these new men were really little more than boys with insufficient education because of the war and considerably underfed and undisciplined. It was the Sergeants' job along with Frank to knock them into shape and turn them into proper soldiers. Of this, an unnamed Essex officer has said:

> "*Unquestionably, the bulk of recruits who flocked to join the Army immediately after the war were young ...*" but adding: "*Yet the fact remains – and here is where the rebels made their mistake - that during those first two years in Ireland those young and physically weak boys grew up and became strong men; and, moreover, by degrees they became disciplined. At the beginning of 1921 they were a force to be reckoned with.*" (Burrows: 270)

There was a constant military traffic of men both joining and leaving and this kept RSM Frank extremely busy on the parade ground and in organising training. The training and other normal 1st Battalion activities were consistently interrupted by the "Sinn Feiners". The 1st Battalion were on constant alert. Money to and from the bank required an armed escort, local parades and band marches were banned. The rebels were always after arms and on one occasion three soldiers travelling on a train were attacked and their rifles stolen.

Percival

During the year 1920, RSM Frank was serving with the battalion's Intelligence Officer Major (later Lt-General) Arthur Percival, with whom he occasionally played tennis.

The Essex regarded Percival (Picture 9) as an efficient counter-guerrilla officer but he gained a reputation for brutality among the Irish population. The Republican rebels saw him as a torturer calling the men under his command "*The Essex Torture Squad*". IRA leader Tom Barry, wrote "*This officer was easily the most viciously anti-Irish of serving British officers. He was tireless in his attempts*

9. Major Percival

to destroy the spirit of the people." (Barry, 1949) After a Royal Irish Constabulary Sergeant was killed outside Bandon Church in July 1920, he captured Tom Hales, IRA West Cork Brigade Commander and Patrick Harte, the Brigade's QM. The torture and beatings the two men suffered during interrogation resulted in Harte's death.

The IRA placed a £1000 bounty for the death of Percival, a large sum at that time but all attempts to eliminate him failed. In October 1920 Percival, with two officers and 12 men, half of whom were recruits, was ambushed on a pitch black night but although some of the party were killed they drove off the Irish attackers. An assassination squad was sent to London in March 1921 but was thwarted by the police. Back in Ireland, Percival led a raid that killed one of the would-be assassins.

The Crossbarry Incident

In the same month, at Crossbarry, County Cork, the Essex with 1,200 troops encircled the IRA West Cork Flying Column with 104 volunteers under the command of Tom Barry. The Irishmen, adept at guerrilla warfare, split into seven small groups and escaped through the encirclement. Barry later published a detailed first-hand account of the incident in his book.

The British had over 12,000 troops in County Cork during the conflict while Barry's men numbered no more than 110. The Army failed to subdue the IRA Flying Columns and Barry's tactics made West Cork ungovernable. Initially, in the first rebel ambushes captured Essex men were released and told to leave the Republicans alone. These warnings were ignored by the Essex and Barry ordered their shooting on the spot while soldiers from other units were better treated. Doubtless this was the consequence of the actions of Major Percival. Aligned to this is the story, by John O'Sullivan, describing an incident in Bandon that occurred during the same period (see: *Appendix C*). This posting was less than heroic compared with their exploits at Gallipoli and Beaumont Hamel.

At this time RSM Frank was permitted to continue: *"in the RSM service"* beyond 21 years for an undefined period an acknowledgment of his value as an experienced NCO and trainer of recruits. The year 1921 was relatively stable for Frank who spent most of his time supervising various Adjutant's and RSM's parades throughout September and October and a mass parade for the Armistice Day march past with his brother Sergeant Drummer Ernest leading an accompanying drum display. Major Percival played a leading role in one of these parades whilst the band played.

Lunch on Christmas Day 1921 brought an eagerly received issue of beer and Frank calling for three cheers for the COs of the battalion. Later that evening Frank, Ernest, other NCOs and other ranks had a long drinks session in the RSM Quarters.

At the beginning of the following year the married personnel left the quarters although Frank stayed on for a day or two to administer the phased withdrawal from the barracks. On 13th January, there was a drum parade beating the retreat at 16.30 hours led by Sgt Drummer Ernest. In February 1922, the Essex were required to withdraw from Cork completely following the Independence Treaty and so travelled to new quarters at Carrickfergus, near Belfast, in the North. Frank and Rose were billeted there until September when they were posted to Bordon Camp in Hampshire.

In January 1923, Frank was again permitted to continue service as RSM beyond 21 years: *"for an undefined period"* and this was followed by the granting of a commission as Lt QM at Warley Barracks. So he had finally and deservedly made it into the officers' ranks.

Further postings followed, to Colchester Garrison (1925), during which time there was increased mechanisation of the battalion and then to Pembroke Dock (1929). Promotion to Captain occurred in 1931 and then to Brevet Major in 1934.

An important assignment was when he accompanied his battalion to the Saar as a member of the League of Nations supervision force for the 1935 Plebiscite that decided its re-entry into Germany. Whilst there, the Essex men observed with some alarm the antics of the Nazis who paraded around in a threatening manner intimidating the locals. Some of the senior officers of the 1st Battalion felt a serious foreboding about their behaviour and felt that this presaged another imminent war. Indeed on returning home to Warley barracks, one of the senior officers had a nervous breakdown.

Thereafter, Captain Frank remained with his regiment residing at home in Warley Hill until promoted to the rank of Major on 1st April 1936 and retiring as Major (QM) from the Essex Regiment on 12th December 1937, the end of a distinguished career in the service of his country. At that time he was the last serving soldier in the regiment holding the South African Medal.

In February 1939 and another war with Germany looming, he was reemployed as an Ordnance Officer attached to an Anti Aircraft Division of the Royal Army Ordnance Corps (RAOC) at Warley Barracks.

In 1941, he was posted to the Anti Aircraft, Ordnance Division to Mill Hill area near Barnet, where there was a gun station, to fill a vacancy for

Ordnance Officer. Both these anti-aircraft postings were primarily for training purposes. On 1st May he completed and signed Army Form B199a, a complete record of army service that summarises all the relevant details of the soldier's career.

On 28th March 1942, he was reengaged to be posted to No.1 Infantry Training Centre (ITC) Essex Regiment, with effect from that date to Mill Hill Area Station again from 3rd April having been granted 42 days notice of leave. Finally, on 8th May Frank was struck off the Strength of No.1, ITC, on completion of the 42 days leave notice and went home. He finally ended his army career aged sixty having joined up at eighteen.

After living the rest of his life quietly, Frank died on 26th January 1956, aged 73 and a third years and is buried with his wife, Rosanne and his son Frederick, my father, in a family grave at Woodman Road Cemetery, Brentwood, Essex (Picture 10).

10. Family Grave in Woodman Road

This appreciation later appeared in 'The Eagle', The Journal of the Essex Regiment (1956):

> "'Bill" Bailey was a fine example of the Old Army which, except for its spirit, almost ceased to exist by the summer of 1915. He was a "proper

Essex calf", and even after many years in" foreign parts" could be quite fluent in the dialect when it suited him.

He was one of the best Regimental Sergeant Majors I have ever met. Not only did he look the part but he was physically and morally courageous. When the 44th came to Bordon after three years' "bushwacking" in Ireland and the Kaiser's War, he did much towards raising drill, discipline and turnout to the pre-war standard. How well he succeeded can be judged from the photographs of the Battalion marching past at the King's Review at Aldershot. Later, I found him to be a most efficient Quartermaster and always helpful, if properly approached. I know too, from personal experience, what he did to boost rifle shooting in the Battalion.

Very "regimental" he could be much on his dignity if necessary, especially if he sensed a slight, however small, on "my Battalion". Once, when he was RSM, a tactless junior Officer, recently transferred from another regiment, made some remark on guard mounting which Bill regarded as a reflection on the 44th. Almost before the offender knew he had transgressed he found himself in front of the Commanding Officer.

He was dined out before leaving to take over Quartermaster at the Depot. It was an event typical of the Army and ended with "Old Bill" being carried around by the Subalterns before being deposited outside his house quite overcome by the reception he had been given.

Now he has left us for good. But we do not forget.'

That eulogy, by Brigadier Frederick A. S. Clarke, D.S.O. who served as a Lieutenant with 1st Essex in Ireland from 1919-22, succinctly sums up the soldier, my grandad.

5.

From Farmer's Sons to Military Men

WHEN I started to chase up the story of my grandad Frank's military career in earnest it never occurred to me that he had any brothers or sisters. As said, whilst living with my grandparents during my youth none ever appeared or were even mentioned.

However, two big surprises awaited me. First, from the military records, elder brother Ernest was discovered to be in the same Essex 1st Battalion. Then at TNA, tumbling out of the 19th century Census paperwork, was a typical Victorian working class family of ten siblings. Apart from Frank (1882-1956) and Ernest Edward (1877-1970), they were: Sarah Harriet (1864-1950), Joseph (1866-unknown), Charles Porter (1871-1950), Elizabeth (1872-1955), Herbert Robert (1874-unknown), Edgar Harvey (1876-1917), Henry Frederick (1880-1927) and Albert (1886-unknown).

At first, it seemed possible that other brothers could have served in the army but there are no records of this.

The Mystery Brother

There was a mystery about Charles, the second son. This followed a trawl through some very old photos mailed to me by Jane, one of which showed a young man in uniform taken at Warley, Brentwood (Picture 6, page 58) and marked as Charles. Checking with the ERM, I discovered that the uniform was that of the specialist MI sent to fight in the Anglo-Boer War between 1899 and 1902 and was taken sometime before 1903.

Here was a mystery.

However, the inevitable rigorous follow-up search through the 'burnt' microfilm records that survived the air raid in 1940 at TNA showed absolutely no evidence of any army service by Charles. Perhaps his records were among those burnt in the fire?

Then, bang! It suddenly hit me. At the time of the photo, Charles was already thirty years old whereas on much closer scrutiny the uniformed man clearly looked a lot younger, not more than twenty at the most. Not only that but, as we saw in the previous account of his army career, Frank had definitely served with the MI during the Boer War, having just enlisted at aged eighteen, so it had to be him instead.

This was a confusing twist in the tale of the Baileys' military service and further alerted me to the problems of authenticating available evidence to a satisfactory degree of certainty. The initial labelling of the photograph was a mistake.

Happily, there was another source to verify this. Ernest's elder daughter Doris, who is alive and well, was sure that Charles was never in the army. It had never been mentioned by her father or anyone in the family and also she said the physical resemblance was not right. It was confirmed as Frank.

Of course it is just possible that, like many other young men looking for alternatives to the dull routines of village life, Charles may have volunteered for the Essex Militia.

If so, it would have been in the 1890s during his twenties. Without any written record of such service it was a dead end and besides which it was mainly the tale of Frank's career I was chasing.

Nevertheless it seems right that Charles deserves a mention here because he features significantly in the affairs of the Bailey family. He appears as next-of-kin, with Joseph the eldest who emigrated to USA, and Ernest on Frank's history sheet and also again on an army career summary, which refers to Major Frank Bailey: *"formerly The Essex Regiment re-employed with RAOC"* on 1st May 1941. He was clearly important as a referee and signatory. He is also influential elsewhere with other siblings and we can see that he obviously kept in frequent touch with his elder sister Sarah Harriet, who was in domestic service, as the postcard from 1913 suggests (Picture 11, next page).

He was the entrepreneurial brother who owned both a shop and a hotel in Belvedere and in the photo postcard of the hotel (Picture 12) his name, C P Bailey, can just be discerned over the entrance. By all accounts, he was also generous to his siblings and their offspring with his obvious wealth. In later life he often used to call on Sarah's son Joseph Firmin and take his family up

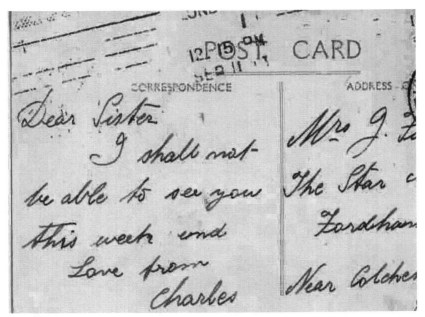

11. Charles' postcard

to Aldeburgh in Suffolk for Sunday tea with salmon sandwiches, which in those days was quite a treat.

He married Martha Caye, a German from Hamburg, on 6th June 1896 and she predeceased him on 3rd December 1935, him marrying again later

12. Charles' Hotel

13. Charles and Emily Bailey

(Picture 13). They are both buried in the churchyard of All Saints Church in Fordham, Essex.

The Regimental Brother

Ernest Edward, the fifth son, was the first surprise relative to emerge clearly on the detection radar. Like Charles, Ernest appeared as next of kin on Frank's enlistment papers. Ernest was already in the Essex Regiment having enlisted on 22nd February 1897, at Colchester, his age stated as follows: "*Apparent (handwritten above) Age: 18 years and 3 months*". This is very interesting because having been born in September 1877 he was nineteen years and five months! There is no way now to fathom this discrepancy but perhaps it supports an earlier point made about how the listener interprets the speaker.

He gave his occupation as a "*Driver*" and was allocated the number 4810. Throughout his army career, he mainly served with the 1st Battalion, the same one Frank joined four years later. He too was involved with them at all the main points of the Great War Campaigns.

Being in the very same battalion was a positive link rather like the Pals' units specifically recruited from close knit localities to form a tight bond between the men and give mutual support. However, this was not invariably the case in all units. Despite their sibling relationship they did not regularly knock around or drink together because they were of different ranks, Frank being slightly ahead in the seniority game. The army categorically disapproved of men of different ranks drinking together as this was held to be bad for discipline. Usually a newly appointed NCO would be sent to another Company to avoid the temptation of being too familiar with his old drinking mates. This particularly applied to relatives. This is evident in both their records where there were many changes between companies in that battalion, as we have seen when Frank was briefly posted to 2nd Bn before eventually going to India to rejoin the 1st Bn.

Not long after enlisting, Ernest was posted to Burma to serve in the Indian part of the British Army for two and a half years from October 1898 until being transferred to India at the end of February 1901 just before younger brother Frank enlisted. He was then posted to South Africa on 6th December 1901 having also been trained in the MI for deployment against the Boers. There is no actual mention of his part in South African actions but we do know about the battalion and its role in the campaign as outlined elsewhere. Like all those who served in that war, Ernest was awarded The Queen's South Africa Campaign Medal with clasps.

He was then transferred from South Africa back to India on 15th August 1902 staying there and again accruing Indian service in that country for four more years. During that time, in 1904, he became a Drummer for the regiment and extended his service to complete 12 years with the colours. This life involved many postings back and forth between these colonial regions as shown by this sequence: posted to Burma in December 1906, back to India in February 1908 for six months as British service, signed up to complete the full term of 21 years to create a life out of professional soldiering, appointed L-Cpl, then more Indian service until November 1913 when the battalion was sent for a stint in the Indo-Colonial relief operation in Mauritius until late 1914. On 7th December 1914, he returned with the Mauritius half of 1st Battalion to Warley Barracks to form up with the rest of the regiment ready for the European theatre of war.

Throughout that time he featured in the July 1909 ERG as L-Cpl in B Company 1st Battalion receiving the "*3rd Class Education Certificate of 18th February 1909 with 153 marks*" and was also photographed in Quetta in

1911 as a Corporal (Acting) in the Regimental Hockey Team. Other entries included him being promoted to Corporal in November 1913 and unpaid Lance-Sergeant (L-Sgt) in January 1914.

Brothers in Action

Like Sgt Frank, L-Sgt Ernest was landed at Cape Helles in W Company on W Beach to reinforce the Lancashire Fusiliers on the first day of the action. The brothers were both responsible for each of their platoons. More details of that day's action are included in the chapter *Gallipoli*.

Later in the campaign, on 9th May 1915, Ernest was wounded in the arm by a gunshot as recorded in the Battalion War Diary as follows: "*Remained in position. Continuous sniping all day. Shelled at dusk and at intervals during the night. Received message that we were to be relieved but no relief came except for 1 Company. W Company retired to the rear for a rest.*" He and his men had to stay in a dangerous and exposed position and he was hit by one of the Turkish snipers. The medics on the site wanted to remove his arm as it had gone black but a Royal Army Medical Corps (RAMC) Captain told him that he would keep his arm and sent him to a field hospital. He returned to England for six to eight weeks to recuperate. That RAMC officer undoubtedly saved his arm.

After his recuperation, he was later promoted to Sergeant on 4th June 1915 and then, from 21st August, spent time with the 3rd Battalion at Tring in Hertfordshire. During that period, Ernest worked on the drum unit, earning this testimonial on 16th March 1916, from CO Major Henderson: "*I am very sorry to lose him, as he has brought the 'Drums' up to a very high state of efficiency. This entailed a lot of hard work as there were only recruits available to form the 'Drums'*". Thereafter, on 24th May, he rejoined the 1st Battalion which was with the BEF in France.

In June 1916 Ernest was appointed Sgt Drummer to the 1st Bn and then immediately joined the battalion in the field in France ready for the first attack at Beaumont Hamel. Shortly afterwards he sustained a shrapnel injury in the back. Strangely, although a living relative says this wound bothered him for the rest of his life there is no record of it in his MOD records.

Having survived The Somme, Ernest spent the rest of the war with the battalion in France until 2nd May 1919. His long war service ensured that at the end of the war he was awarded the 1914-15 Star, the British War and Allied Victory Medals as a Sergeant, the inscription "*Sergeant Drummer*" (the 1881-1928 title of the Drum Major) being struck through in the Medal Roll.

14. *Ernest Bailey's Army Character Certificate*

He received the Meritorious Service Medal under Army Order 338 of 1919, this award appearing in *The London Gazette* for 12th December 1919 and was also entitled to the Long Service and Good Conduct Medals. He remained in the army until 1923 and was renumbered along with the rest of the army in mid-1920 at which time he was the second longest serving man, receiving the new number 5998002 under the reorganised system.

He appeared on the Absent Voters Lists (the electoral roll for the overdue election) in the spring and autumn of 1919 as entitled to vote from Fossetts Road, Fordham. His next of kin was given as *"Father, H Bailey, of Fordham"* although clearly this was his mother Harriet's initial, yet another sign of interpretational problems in the official information recorded by the clerk.

He was discharged from Warley Barracks on 31st August 1923 as a Sgt Drummer with Conduct "Exemplary" having claimed his discharge at three months notice, receiving the pension of 47½d per day (nearly four old shillings and now 20p in today's currency) from 1st September 1923. He had served for 26 years and six months. His Character Certificate on leaving is a glowing statement attesting to his positive attitudes and behaviour, especially towards those in his charge, as shown (Picture 14, previous page). Given the size of this reproduction, the age of this original document and the distinctive writing style of the period it requires clear deciphering.

It says: *"Is honest sober and trustworthy. Intelligent, holds 2nd Class Cert of Education dated 12.6.11. Promoted L/C. 27.10.08. Cpl. 25.11.13. Sgt. 4.6.15. Sgt Drummer 1.6.16.*

> *I cannot speak too highly of this N.C.O. He possesses initiative & common sense. Whilst enforcing strict discipline among those under him he is most popular with all ranks. His first care has always been the welfare of those committed to his charge. I confidently recommend him to any employer. Trade before enlisting. Driver. J Moffatt, Lt Colonel, Commanding 1st Batt The Essex Regiment."*

Ernest did not marry until very late in life. Whatever the reason for this delay it is most likely to have been his Great War experiences. He met twenty year old Violet Irene Truman, the daughter of a retired policeman who ran a local pub in Fordham and married her, aged 51 in 1929 at Colchester. Unfortunately, Violet, who had some heart and chest problems, predeceased Ernest in 1965 but they had two daughters, Doris born in 1929 and Irene, born in 1931. He joined the Home Guard in WW2 and died in 1970, aged 92, the longest living descendant of Joseph and Harriet Bailey.

15. Ernest in old age

Doris told me that my grandad Frank was her favourite uncle and both he and Ernest had a wicked sense of humour which kept her laughing. Ernest is shown in ripe old age with his favourite pipe (Picture 15).

The Unknown Brother

After the discovery of Ernest being in the same battalion the military chase was on a big roll. However, the initial elation of that untoward discovery turned quickly into frustration. Another ERM enquiry revealed that yet another of Frank's elder brothers had also served in the army. Edgar Harvey Bailey, the fourth son, proved to be, and stubbornly remained, very much an enigma.

At the time of this startling discovery, there was an almost complete lack of available information about him apart from the tantalisingly slim ERM outline data. So it was off to TNA again but, strangely, there was not a single trace of him in the army files. Surely his files were not burnt in the 1940 air raid as well? If so, that would be double bad luck for my search.

From the ERM data, I learned that Edgar enlisted at Colchester Garrison although not in the same regiment as his brothers. There was no obvious reason why he enlisted with the Royal Field Artillery (RFA), at the time one of three branches of the divided Royal Artillery in 1899. Was it because he wanted to make his own mark in the military world independent of his

16. *Edgar Bailey in Royal Field Artillery Uniform*

brothers? Perhaps there had been some sibling or family disagreement?

It remains undocumented. This is the frustrating side of this task. What we do know is that like Ernest, he also gave his occupation as a "*Driver*", which before mechanised gun movements really meant horse handler. This was clearly an ideal job for a farmer's son.

In the 1901 Census, he was recorded as living in Fordham as an "*Ordinary Farm Labourer*" with his wife Eva, née Bunton, whom he married on 14th December the year before. The ERM had him living in West Bergholt, about four miles from Colchester, although this seems to have been later. Edgar shown in uniform (Picture 16) was in the 47th Division Ammunition Column, RFA, and was active in the Great War. The records then had him having died of wounds on 13th August 1917, sustained at an unknown location somewhere in France or Belgium and buried in a place called Loker.

He is also commemorated on a memorial in the New St Mary the Virgin Church, West Bergholt, Essex. *The Essex Chronicle* Newspaper for 21st September 1917 recorded his death as did *The Times* of 15th September 1917. His widow Eva was left with three children: Nellie, Oliver, Albert. Oliver died at 23, probably of TB, and is buried in All Saints Churchyard, Fordham.

Where and how did he die? Was it France or Belgium? What kind of wound caused his death? Early in the search, there was no available record of exactly where or how he was wounded nor was there any indication of any time span between that and him dying of those wounds. That time span could be anything between hours, weeks and months depending upon the severity of the injury and that was unknown. What was known was that he was transported back from the front, admitted and treated by sisters at Loker Hospice in the small village of the same name, about three miles west of Ypres.

17. Edgar's Grave in Loker, Flanders

Being buried at that location, the strong suspicion pointed to his unit being part of 3rd Ypres, better and more notoriously known as Passchendaele. I had to find his grave and anything else to unravel the largely invisible life of this recently discovered great uncle. On visiting Loker his grave was found in a small beautifully kept low walled cemetery in a field just behind the main village street and across the road from the Hospice (Picture 17). Paying due respect to the only known family member to die in that war and whose existence was only discovered a few months beforehand was truly emotional and rewarding. The serenity at that spot on that cold but bright afternoon was immensely humbling.

Despite the emotional rush at having traced a real artefact and added some sort of substance to his story it still looked like a difficult trail. As it was, with Edgar at rest in Loker, it seemed a fair guess it was more likely he died in nearby Flanders rather than distant France.

Whilst in the area I discovered The Passchendaele Archives who are constructing a database about any relative fighting or dying there in 1917. On returning home, I sent Edgar's details such as I had in return for any information about his death. Another metaphorical flash had been instigated but would it produce a successful informational bang? Much time passed and the Edgar trail stayed as cold as the oncoming autumnal weather. It looked like his secret would have to remain buried with him. Then, out of the blue it came: another long awaited bang via email.

Edgar was in the RFA, 47th Division Ammunition Column, which itself was incorporated as part of the 140th Brigade of the 47th London Division. This division was relieved from the front in the Ypres Salient on 8th August 1917 but the 140th Brigade stayed behind to keep the defences solid and provide close artillery support to X Corps who were attacking the Hollebeke area, south of Ypres. The field artillery was positioned one or two miles behind the frontline in the area north of Wijtschaete and Oosttaverne.

An artillery brigade was strung out along a couple of miles of road when on the move and was obviously vulnerable to any enemy crossfire. Edgar was a lorry driver, servicing the unit, when to quote Volume II of the War Diary: "*Aug13. Hostile plane at 11.30am dropped bomb on No. 2 Section lines wounding 3 OR's (1 died), 2 LD killed, 3 LD wounded.*" So, one of the three OR's (Other Ranks) died along with two of the three LD (Lorry Drivers) of which Edgar was one, either there and then or later that day.

Edgar was awarded the Victory and British War Medals after his death. These medals were sent to his widow. He rests in peace with honour in a Flanders field where he fought bravely for his country.

Coincidentally but unfortunately his brother Frank was later gassed in the battle at Langemarck literally just a couple of miles up the road but thankfully survived the experience.

6.

Gallipoli

DAWN IS breaking over the Aegean Sea on Cape Helles at the tip of the Gallipoli Peninsula on Sunday 25th April 1915. The morning air is still, there is no wind, the sea is calm, "*smooth as glass*" we are told, greenish in colour and there is no discernable sign of life on the shore. The remains of an early morning mist drifts and swirls unevenly about the peninsula giving it an eerie stillness that pervades the immediate area despite the big guns sounding further up the straits.

Having sailed slowly all night from the Greek island of Mudros, the British troopship 'Dongola' is approaching the Turkish coastline. Aboard it, Captain (later Major) John Gillam, Army Service Corps (ASC), is making notes in his Gallipoli Diary (1918)[1]. He writes: "*Was awaked at 4am by the noise of the distant rumbling of guns, and coming to my senses I realised that the great effort had started.*" Indeed it has. This is the first day of the Gallipoli land campaign and the naval bombardment has already begun.

A look at the map (Picture 18), shows Cape Helles arrowed which is located at the entrance to The Dardanelles, a 40 mile narrow strip of water leading to the Sea of Marmara and the Bosphorus Strait at the Turkish capital Istanbul (then Constantinople). Dividing European and Asian Turkey, this waterway is the only route linking the Black Sea to the Aegean and Mediterranean Seas and so is vitally important both in commercial and military terms. Given its geographical position, it is no surprise that many historic campaigns have been fought to gain control of the peninsula for strategic advantage. This Allied effort is yet another such campaign.

Looking back to before this day, there has been intense and drawn-out discussion as to whether the 29th Division, including the 1st Essex Regiment

18. Gallipoli Peninsula Map (arrow showing Cape Helles)

(1st Essex) as part of 88th Brigade, should be posted to France or the Middle East. It is decided upon the latter. It is to be Gallipoli. They are chosen to make a difficult landing on, and seize the peninsula to facilitate an advance on the Turkish capital. The 1st Essex, a thousand strong, set off on 21st March and, as they embark for Alexandria, an officer of the Royal Scots in Burrows (1931) describes the Essex men as: "*Magnificent men, tall, well-built and trained to the moment.*" In the event they would need to be.

After much practice at landing against opposition both on board and in Alexandria Harbour, the 1st Essex is prepared for action.

At dawn on the 25th, just before the attack actually begins, Capt Gillam observes the Essex men lining up in good order at dawn on the ship's deck showing no discernable fear. His army experience is shown by the way he describes the 'fall in', worth quoting at length as he succinctly captures the preparations for the landings: "*I dressed hastily, went on deck, and there found the Essex and Royal Scots falling in on parade, with full packs, two bags of iron rations and the unexpended portion of the day's rations (for they had breakfasted), entrenching tools, 200 rounds of ammunition, rifle and bayonet. I stood and watched their faces, listened to what they said to each other, and could trace no sign of fear in their faces and no words of apprehension at forthcoming events in their conversation. It was a simple 'fall in' just as of old in the days of peace parades, with familiar faces of their NCOs and officers before them like one big family party ... the booming of the guns grows louder.*"

However, appearances under pressure are variable and often deceptive. Unless actually there or having first-hand experience of combat, we can never ever know in any meaningful way what goes through men's minds just before a dangerous military action. Showing no obvious fear may be interpreted in different ways. People who are apprehensive or scared often give a good impression of being outwardly calm and may engage in light-hearted banter even appearing to be blasé. The regular professionals among them, especially the experienced NCOs, including my grandfather Frank who has been in the Boer War, behave in a routine or even ritual manner. He helps to reassure and impart confidence to the volunteer recruits preparing for their first ever action.

Despite Gillam's observations of their demeanour, the raw recruits are naturally scared but are trying very hard to keep up appearances because they do not want to let their pals down by panicking and freezing. For those like me, with Frank and his elder brother Ernest there and wishing to know what it was like for them in the thick of the mayhem, we are fortunate that John Gillam has recorded his observations and insights for posterity which give a close-up complement to the larger history of that ill-fated campaign.

On that first morning of the beach landings, 'HMS Albion' starts the preliminary naval bombardment at 05.00 hours creating a huge background din, initially described by Gillam. Later, 'HMS Queen Elizabeth' unleashes

19. Setting off for the beaches

her 15" guns, one now ensconced at the entrance of the Imperial war Museum (IWM).

The first landings are scheduled for 05.30 hours. The troops for the landings are to be taken by the ships as close to the shore as they safely can without drawing howitzer fire. The next phase is to be taken towards the beaches directly in motorised cutters or towed by 'pinnaces' (tugboats) in 'lighters' (flat bottomed open boats) roped together towards land (Picture 19). As they near the shore they are cast off to be rowed the last part to the beaches.

The intended objectives for the various infantry units are certain beaches designated by the letters: S, V, W, X and Y. They are to capture the cape of this peninsula by landing and linking up with other detachments to form a bigger bridgehead and thus enable an advance towards the Turkish capital.

However, having been alerted to the allies' intentions by the previous naval bombardment in the Dardanelles Straits, the Turkish defences have been considerably reinforced in the last few weeks. The result for the 1st Lancashire Fusiliers proves to be devastating (see: Background, below).

Essex Landing

The men of the 1st Essex are initially allocated to land on Y beach, which it later transpires is occupied without resistance. They are diverted by a last minute change of command decision to reinforce the Lancashire Fusiliers on W Beach. From the troopship, Gillam notes: "*We hear the Lancashires have landed there and are a few hundred yards inshore fighting for dear life.*" Indeed it transpires they have gained a slender foothold on it but are pinned down by a constant hail of small arms fire and are hanging on by sheer courage.

The 1st Lancashire CO, Major H R Bishop records the Essex landing in his Intelligence Report: "*10am. Essex Regt reinforced on our right.*" It is unclear whether this means the Essex landing on the beach or ready to do battle. In battle situations, specific timings of actions are rarely synchronised owing to the obvious confusion involved. Here, there are different versions because of the time it takes to row and steer the boats to shore, disembark under withering fire and hit the beach to take up a position. Either way it is clear from this commander's Intel report that 1st Essex are on W beach early that first morning reinforcing the Lancashire battalion and Frank Bailey is there with them.

When the Essex men approach the cape in the open boats they are now vulnerable to enemy machine gun and sniper fire. These large rowing boats are packed to the gunnels, crammed with loads of brave men plucked from the farms, villages and townships of Essex, some only a year before, and now thrust into this diversionary campaign. Each man has a pick and shovel in addition to his normal kit ready to dig in and consolidate their position. Many of these men are young volunteers sitting apprehensively awaiting their moment of destiny in their first action.

As they near the objective, being rowed all too slowly for comfort into this barren rocky and alien peninsula with machine gun emplacements in the hills and bluffs overlooking the beaches, thoughts of home and family left behind cross their minds. Now they must remove any distractions. However much combat experience they have all soldiers hate the wait more than getting stuck into the action. As many veterans testify, they try to counteract any emotions produced in this dreadful waiting period by collecting their thoughts and deliberately focussing on the task ahead. Once battle starts there is no time to dwell on any inner feelings which are blocked out by the noise and confusion.

20. Rowing boats towed in for beach landings

Each boat has a rowing detail, some naval and others army and an officer with pistol and whistle. Picture 20 shows these small boats being towed in towards the beaches and one of the towing tugs is steaming back towards the troopships on the horizon. Frank Bailey, now a Sgt, sits crouched in one of these boats in charge of his troop as does his elder brother Ernest elsewhere. Their job is that of the middle man between the commanding officer and the men and this task is crucial in conflict. Clear communication between them all is a must as is tight discipline under enemy fire. Following orders when one's senses say the opposite is the basis of their military training.

They have consistently trained in landing drills on the voyage over from Egypt to achieve this very task today. After all the drills the time has come for the real thing. As they approach the shore, Frank is alert and outwardly calm to his men, reassuring them and inspiring morale for the task ahead. They must now remain keenly focussed under fire for to lose concentration is to invite disaster to both themselves and their troop.

Even in the early morning sunshine, the Gallipoli coastline is forbidding. It is a barren landscape with little or no features or trees that can provide essential cover. There it is: the objective. This is the very narrow W Beach. It's only a quarter of a mile long at most and at times only 15 feet across. Overlooking the beach and immediately above – hanging over it almost – are steep rocky slopes, a scarp or bluff varying in height but mostly about 40-60 feet high.

Beyond the beach it has been established there is some open ground suitable for a camp. It will be a very difficult landing. This high open ground is ideal for the defenders and makes a perfect terrain for a stout defence with machine gun emplacements and some light artillery. Achi Baba, the nearby dominant promontory is controlled by the Turks who can see for many miles around and so it is ideal ground for them but definitely not the ideal beachhead for the Essex men.

Frank's Company

Initially, despite what has happened earlier to the Lancashire men, the leading Company of 1st Essex to reach the beach gets onto the front part under lighter fire and with fewer casualties. Strangely, the photograph of the battalion landing (Picture 21), with the words 'dead' and 'Lizzie' (HMS Queen Elizabeth just behind the hill), actually belies what is really happening elsewhere or what is about to happen here.

It does not and it cannot possibly capture the reality of their plight: the blazing heat of the sun, the dust, the noise and the obvious threat. Incredibly, it has the air of a Sunday afternoon archaeological society gathering rather than an organised expedition of men trying to consolidate their position in a dangerous conflict location under the eyes of the enemy. However, it does seem to support Gillam's previous observation of the men: "*... like one big family party*". Note the barren landscape with no cover for the exposed troops soon to be under enemy fire from the cliff on the right and the lack of helmets.

As the Turkish defenders realise the battalion is attempting to reinforce the occupation of the beachhead the situation quickly changes. Increasing firepower erupts as they concentrate their aim onto the boats, the beach as well as farther out to sea. Like the Lancashire battalion earlier, many men from the next Essex boats are picked off as they scramble ashore. Some are even hit even before they leave the towboats. Eventually they will make it to some basic cover and link up with the remnants of the earlier battalions at the prearranged collection point.

As X Company, under Capt Pepys and Sgt Bailey, are about to set off in the small boats to take them to the shore, Capt Pepys distinctly hears a shouted order to the "middy" (midshipman) in charge of the 'pinnace' towing the boats, to aim well to starboard to avoid the underwater barbed wire defences and the mines. This diversion helps that company who are able to avoid the sunken wire and step directly onto the shore. On doing so they too are met by fierce enemy firepower but fortunately no one is wounded.

21. Snapshot of 1st Battalion Essex landing on W Beach

They are followed immediately by Lt-Col Godfrey-Faussett and the HQ staff. They are all instructed to get inshore and mount the cliff as quickly as possible. The fire from the all the cliffs remains constant. Despite the impression given in Picture 21, obviously taken without any defensive fire, the 1st Essex men are badly exposed on open ground with no obvious protection under the now blazing sunshine. Any safety can only come from how quickly they can take cover under the bluffs and secure the cliff tops. An Essex Sergeant wryly notes: *"There was only one hotter place than that was, and that was not heaven!"* (Burrows)[2]

Once across the beach, this company manages to make it some way up the incline towards the redoubt at the top but they come under another severe torrent of firepower. They drop and crawl into a damaged and deserted Turkish trench to gain cover. This shallow trench does not provide any real protection and ironically those outside it are better off despite the sniper fire. Eventually, a detachment copes with the defensive onslaught and a vital link is finally made with the beleaguered remnants of the Lancashire men. Whilst the general din of battle is deafening around them and bullets seem to be coming from everywhere the men of this company are still far from securely positioned.

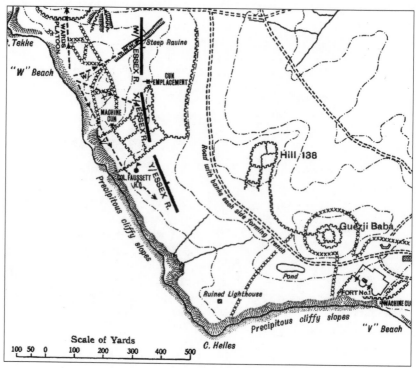

22. *1st Battalion Essex position at W Beach, morning of 25th April*

Capt Churchill of Y Company understates this in his account: *"There seemed to be a deuce lot of lead flying about. The view of the beach looked most unappetizing."* (Burrows) Precisely, they must make protective cover soonest. There is a clearly defined objective and that is Hill 138 about 500 yards inland as shown on the map (Picture 22, previous page). Y Company needs to meet up with the others which it does after some scrabbling in the dirt up the hill towards the redoubt. Later on, the Essex men are now with the other units who are to their left and right and have achieved the first stage of their reinforcement orders.

Now, X and Y Companies, along with Frank, have to take the redoubt but are again held up by heavy defensive fire. Just then, shells from a battleship blitz the enemy position and they are now able to advance to the very top. Finally, at 14.15 hours, the Essex seizes and secures the redoubt on Hill 138. In his diary, Capt Gillam says: *"2.15pm. I hear a cheer, a real British one. Is that a charge?"* then giving a graphic firsthand account of the action: *"What I see is crouching figures, some almost bent double, others jogtrotting over the grass with bright sun rays flashing on their bayonets. Now and again a figure falls and lies still – very still in a crumpled heap; while all the time the crack-crack of musketry and the pop-popping of machine guns never cease."*

Hill 138 becomes the Battalion HQ for the night. The Essex and the other units have finally prevailed and they get to eat their first meal of the day: bully beef, biscuits and loads of tea.

AFTERMATH
Krithia

After resting up for a day, the next objective was Krithia village some four miles away. This engagement proved to be a see-saw affair with advances being counteracted and eventually failing. In fact, there were three battles of Krithia. This was particularly galling because certain officers had virtually strolled into it on the first day when the way was clear from Y Beach, as was the road to Achi Baba. Opportunity lost and the game was over before it started except no one grasped this unpalatable fact at the time.

On 1st May, the battalion went into Reserve but was quickly called up to the front again to plug a gap at midnight and the following day to repel a very heavy 10,000 strong Turkish counterattack along the whole line. Capt Pepys and Sgt Frank Bailey engaged in a rapid bayonet charge which helped to stem the enemy effort. Once again the men were then posted into reserve only to be recalled to action yet again.

This incessant contrast between action and counteraction again carried on throughout May and June with the 1st Essex constantly digging trenches at which they excelled. It was during this time that Frank's elder battalion brother Ernest was wounded in the shoulder in a barely protected trench on 9th May. Without specific individual details, save the regimental record, it is clear Frank and Ernest were both involved with their companies at the very centre of most of the action for the rest of the campaign. As well as being involved in the fierce battles for Krithia, they were involved a week later in the diversionary tactics at Suvla Bay further up the coast as part of the early August offensives in the north of the peninsula.

Suvla Bay

At the Suvla Bay landing it first appeared that lessons have been learned from the disastrous lost opportunities in the first days at Gallipoli. The action started at 21.30 hours under cover of the impending darkness (Picture 23) and every effort was made to soundproof movement of equipment. It worked, for by 22.00 hours 3,000 men were ashore without a shot being fired. It was a brilliant improvement on the landings in April. Once again though, it was the commanders who missed the big opportunity of seizing the higher ground in time. In the long run, this action again showed up the lack of direct involvement of C-in-C Hamilton, who stayed on Imbros awaiting news and the incompetent inexperience of the CO on the ground, Lt-General Stopford, who had never even been in charge of a large army formation and did not even set foot on the site, remaining instead on board a navy vessel.

23. Approaching Suvla Bay at dusk

With supreme irony, after the failure to achieve the long term goal the eventual evacuation of the Gallipoli Peninsula was, by contrast, the most successful part of the campaign. It was impeccably planned and successfully applied the vital ingredient that had been lacking at the outset: the element of secrecy and surprise. It was a smoothly conducted operation with its stealthy night time manoeuvring which removed the majority of the force from the beachheads without any recordable losses. Many tactics were used to fool the Turks into thinking that the allies were there for the duration, such as the self-firing rifles or the troops appearing to vanish for an hour or so and then firing on them as they emerged to inspect trenches. In one case, soldiers played daily cricket matches in the face of possible enemy fire with great aplomb on the beach giving a clear impression of permanence.

Throughout this campaign, Frank and Ernest were both engaged with the 1st Battalion Essex, as part of the MEF, from 23rd March 1915 until posted to France on 21st March 1916, just before the great Somme offensive in which they were to play another important part with their comrades.

24. 1st Battalion Essex Gallipoli survivors in 1918

The 1st Bn had played a crucial role on that first day, reinforcing the Lancashire Fusiliers at a key point of the W beach landing. Yet in the subsequent historical record their contribution is glossed over in comparison. The photograph (Picture 24) shows Capt Paxton, M.C. and the 1st Bn Gallipoli survivors on Armistice Day 1918. RSM/WO 1 Frank Bailey is sitting, far right in the second row. If one counts these men it is clear they paid a heavy price in Gallipoli given that the battalion started out with a thousand men.

BACKGROUND

The context of the Gallipoli campaign was the problem faced by the Western Allies after the first year of the war which had become stuck in a stalemate, referred to as 'trench lock'. Inspired by Winston Churchill, First Lord of the Admiralty, the Allies sought to break this deadlock by diverting the focus of the war effort through the back door against Turkey. This would achieve several results.

First, it would knock Turkey, widely perceived to be the weak link of the enemy, out of the war and so activate much needed movement in this theatre to counteract the stagnation in France and Belgium.

Second, it would leave Germany and Austria-Hungary exposed in their Mediterranean underbelly. As a result they would be forced to divert troops to the Mediterranean which would weaken their Western front which could be opened up again.

Third, opening up this vital waterway would allow much-needed two-way traffic between Russia and the Western allies. Indirectly, the pressure would also be off Egypt and some of the Balkan states may have been encouraged to join the allies.

The initial strategy was to have the British and French navies sail up the Dardanelles Straits, bombard the shore batteries and to boldly arrive outside Constantinople forcing the Turks to surrender. Given that official strategy, it is ironic that it is replicated by Capt Gillam in his diary Preface as his personal hope: "*I heard that the Division (29th) was bound for the Dardanelles instead of France at an early date. I knew that in all probability the division was destined to play a most romantic part in the Great War. I had visions of trekking up the Gallipoli Peninsula with the navy bombarding a way for us up the straits and along the coastline to the Sea of Marmara until after a brief campaign we entered triumphantly Constantinople to meet the Russian Army which would link up with ourselves to form part of a great chain encircling and throttling the Central Empires.*" Unfortunately, it did not pan out like this at all.

Conceptually and strategically, the plan had much to commend it. It was bold and imaginative. However, there were several serious problems in the planning stage that ultimately undermined any possible success. It was rushed and therefore failed to attend to important details. The result was serious ineptitude in the tactical aspects of organisation and coordination. This reflected a false ethnocentric arrogance about the superiority of the British Empire and its military with colonial experience over the perceived weakness of Turkey, its lack of commitment to the war and the inability of its troops to fight.

This misplaced overconfident thinking proved to be based on erroneous intelligence and inadequate topographic data which had a disastrous effect on the landings from the very beginning and was the very undoing of the whole campaign. Arrogance with ignorance unnecessarily cost many allied lives. Kitchener believed that twice the number of men allocated would be needed but only half were available for the attack, doubtless owing to the increasing losses and need for replacements on the Western Front. General Sir Ian Hamilton, who had previously made his name as Kitchener's Chief of Staff, was thrust late into the role of C-in-C and strangely not part of the planning process. Also, he was crucially short of artillery and ammunition and there was a dearth of available howitzers and trench mortars. His task was monumental, for as his biographer John Lee (2000) observes: *"Never in human history had his task – an assault landing in the face of an enemy who was prepared and armed with rapid firing weapons – been attempted"*.

In fact, the original conception of the campaign did not involve any landings at all but was designed to use only naval power to silence the on-shore guns on either side of the straits so as to ensure a safe opening up of this channel allowing clear passage to Constantinople and the Black Sea (Picture 25). Long before the eventual April army landings, the naval bombardment of the coastline which had started on 19th February did not initially achieve its objective. Later on, parties of allied army and navy personnel eventually did land and knock out various outer defences. So far, so good! However, despite this early success, subsequent landings met with increasingly fierce resistance.

Despite this early setback, on 18th March, British and French battle-ships sailed up the Narrows and, despite some heavy

25. The naval attacks

losses to both guns and mines, nearly pulled off a startling victory. The Turkish batteries were nearly out of heavy ammunition and the enemy was convinced that an attack would follow the next day. This was merely the first lost opportunity to follow through on an advantage. It was so close and yet so far. Although unknown at the time, later intelligence showed that continuation of this assault would have proved successful. Nevertheless, this demonstrated the poor level of general intelligence that dogged the whole campaign from start to finish. Not only that but Hamilton had only arrived there the day before and remained detached from the action on a separate battleship.

As the allied force attempted to move further up the straits things only got worse. The allied ships had to contend with mines and the mobile batteries from each shore and many were damaged or sunk. The opportunity for such a naval advance was now lost and also any element of strategic surprise long gone. The enemy was now alerted to the probability of a ground attack. It was now handed over to the military to accomplish an invasion and this would start with the beach landings on 25th April. The overall German Commander in charge of Turkish defences, Lt-General Otto Liman von Sanders, realised this was likely and took over the specific supervision of the peninsula and the system of defences was quickly bolstered.

Then the land attack was further delayed for over a month after the naval bombardment because vital equipment needed for landing was at the bottom of the ships' holds and needed to be reloaded for faster access. Von Sanders, quoted in Robert Rhodes James (1999), confirmed this: "*The British allowed us four good weeks of respite for all this work before their great disembarkation.*"

Inevitably, in warfare there is a big gap between planning and execution because in a fast moving and chaotic battle scenario there are always glitches in implementation and things take longer than imagined. This is shown by discrepancies in the different times and placements given for the same troop deployments in the various records. At Gallipoli, from the word go, almost everything that could go wrong did so.

A number of serious problems emerged. Many of the troops to be deployed in this action were inexperienced, particularly some of the colonial soldiers, who had only recently enlisted and were not fully trained at the start of the campaign. Reference maps were sixty years old dating from the Crimean War or in some cases were actually tourist maps! When troops were ordered to take their positions on land they either could not find them relative to their maps or the features themselves were not even there.

There was no supreme commander but separate commanders for the army and navy. The land C-in-C, Hamilton, remained far removed from the action throughout by staying on board his ship. He was timid and indecisive in giving orders to his subordinates. Hunter-Weston, GOC 29th Division, lacked imagination and, being unable to adapt to fast changing circumstances, continuously and carelessly threw men at obviously overwhelming odds. It was Balaclava all over again.

Unlike Hamilton, von Sanders, had an authoritative and direct command over his charges, read the signs and prepared his ground well. During the landings the enemy fire from the shore was well organised and devastatingly accurate. Despite this, many other opportunities were also egregiously lost where landings were completely unopposed and the higher ground was not taken or consolidated. This initially occurred on two beaches and on one of them the gradually rising 200-foot incline was absolutely deserted. This would have made a superbly placed command post but the soldiers sat around all day trying to establish who was in command and waiting for orders from Hunter-Weston that failed to arrive.

In one case, on arriving at Y beach, one CO found that instead of his men being dug in and entrenched in the commanding position overlooking the beaches they were enjoying a swim in the warm waters. Other officers were recorded as having virtually strolled just under two miles into the nearby town of Krithia which was amazingly deserted. Not only that but it was quite near to the commanding 600-foot summit of Achi Baba, with a grandstand view over the peninsula. Control of this point would have undoubtedly swung the attack the allies' way. Without any specific orders from above they returned and the men 'brewed up' at 15.00 and settled for the night. This was yet another lost golden opportunity that later proved immensely costly in soldiers' lives.

Other serious problems occurred in transferring the men from the troopships into the boats to be towed by tugs. This did not go smoothly and in one case there was a costly delay when one of the main ships had to wait for a very long time for the tow boats to get organised and alongside. This resulted in a dangerous immobility which exposed the whole operation to enemy artillery. Many men were wounded or killed even before they had got into the boats. This hold up meant that it was 06.30 hours before those first troops reached X beach. The fact the landings here were initially unopposed did not excuse the wasted time and the lost opportunity to gain and dig in on the higher ground or the lack of clear command.

26. 1st Lancashire Fusiliers on their way

Lancashire Landing

The 1st Lancashire Fusiliers tasted the bitter fruits of this doomed attack in a fulsome way. The Turks had considerably reinforced the beaches at Helles and this was demonstrated devastatingly at W Beach. From the outset, things went very badly for the men from Lancashire who set off at 05.00 hours from the troopship. This transfer from ship to shore via the open landing boats (Picture 26) was tortuously slow and the men were packed into the boats like sardines and in increasing danger from sniper fire the nearer they got to land.

When they were 50 yards from their allotted beach they were cast off and had to row themselves into land and the expected enemy fire. Strangely this did not happen. The defenders were waiting for them to reach the beach before they shot at them so as not to unnecessarily attract any artillery fire from the big battleships moored out to sea. When the Lancashire men reached the shoreline and left their boats to scramble ashore, they immediately ran into intensive fire laid on them my some 100 well placed machine gunners and riflemen. Broad lines of barbed wire entanglements lay below the water line at the water's edge along with mines as well. Many of the men became trapped by the barbed wire and they never even got to the beach. They were caught by enfilading fire[3] and as they struggled to get free, we are told, it literally tore them open so the water literally ran red.

Lancashire CO Major Bishop summarises this in their war diary: "*5.30. Landed under heavy fire from machine guns and rifles from cliffs. Heavy casualties. Several men hit in boats & in water before getting ashore. 9 am. In possession of 114 hill & adjacent redoubts. Barbed wire entanglement near water edge. Dispositions reported to BGC (Brigade General Command).*"

The carnage was unbelievable. Despite their undoubted bravery, the 1030 men of 1st Lancashire Fusiliers, initially undertaking the first landing on W Beach, were reduced to 410 men by dawn of the second day. Later, this particular part of the action entered folklore becoming known as "*Six VCs before breakfast*" and the beach was subsequently named the "Lancashire Landing" in honour of that battalion's unflinching courage against all the odds. It was at this point that Frank's battalion was diverted from its original objective and sent in to help reinforce them eventually helping to establish a position on the headland.

Hindsight

It is easy for us looking back now to sit in judgment but the lesson of history is that to fully understand events we should try to put ourselves in the shoes of those people at that time. Bearing that in mind and with the passing of many years there are a number of points to be addressed.

The foremost factor was that this attack was a 'first'. Never before in military history had men ever attempted an opposed amphibious landing by attacking a coastline defended by industrial weapons: heavy guns, mortars and machine guns. The firm belief among allied troops was that they had faced at least two Turkish divisions whilst landing that first day but it later transpired to their amazement that there were only three battalions opposing them: about 2,100 men. It was an object lesson in how a well chosen strategic defensive system could win out over large numbers.

On that first day, 5,000 men were killed or wounded, many of them from the 1st Essex when reinforcing the 1st Lancashire. The Gallipoli campaign lasted 259 days, from that notoriously chaotic Sunday 25th April 1915, with troops unloading and landing directly exposed to enemy fire, to the far more successful evacuation by 8th January 1916 and sustained 250,000 allied losses.

Something often overlooked was the ferocious heat of the summer weather both in the Aegean Sea and on land. As reported in the private diaries of many on the island of Lemnos (less than 50 miles from the Gallipoli Peninsula) the searing heat was unbearable from sunrise at 05.00 to sundown at 19.00. One unknown man complained that he got sunburned knees so many times that the skin was burnt raw. By contrast it was extremely cold at night often with ground frost in the later months of the campaign. This combination of daytime heat and night time frost meant that the men spent most of their time exposed to unhelpful weather conditions in their narrow and shallow trenches (Picture 27).

27. A Gallipoli Trench

The commanders were unimaginative and indecisive, particularly C-in-C Hamilton. He was clearly not used to the new type of warfare. Some of this was the result of his being appointed in a hurry and not being given what many considered enough troops for the job. On the distaff side he was inadequate for the job because of his distance from the front as opposed to the direct involvement of Von Sanders and Mustafa Kemal, the future leader of the Turkish Republic. The subsequent inability to do anything other than order troops into attacking well dug-in stiff resistance again and again was a forerunner of Haig's similar strategy at the Somme a year later. Clearly, lessons about officer appointments had not been well learned from the Crimea.

The British Army at Gallipoli suffered from a backward looking organisational structure and practice which was increasingly counteracted by a fast moving technological development. Some commentators believe that this campaign occurred at the start of a steep 'learning curve' for the army in adapting to the industrial age of warfare. Whether this curve was even underway at all at Gallipoli is certainly contentious, given the results. It is also a moot point whether this learning had even occurred by the start of The Somme in 1916 where the losses were even worse; being produced by similar outdated thinking and tactics not to mention flawed intelligence.

The troops were clearly courageous but their commanders were hidebound and disorganised. They were unable to adapt to changing and challenging conditions and therefore by adhering to static traditional thinking all this bravery came to nought. As author Sir Michael Howard says, it was: "*Brilliant in conception, lamentable in execution,*" a view fully supported by Field Marshal Bernard Montgomery, the later victor of El Alamein, who says: "*Gallipoli was a daring, imaginative scheme, thrown away because of every conceivable mistake in its execution by the commanders.*" a doubly damning yet true assessment.

As indicated, Gallipoli was an attempt to outflank the trench war on the Western Front but as the men never got more than two miles inland, it merely replicated it. On the narrow beaches with steep, overhanging slopes, in the baking sun or freezing cold, there was no area for relaxing away from the range of artillery (Stevenson: 2004). As a result the men were never fully safe in many of the ad-hoc shallow trenches and inadequate dug outs on the sloping hillocks some of which were only 15 yards from the enemy trenches.

Despite some attempts to bolster these and make them safer there was always the danger of partial exposure to accurate sniper fire from the higher ground where the Turks had a well constructed and secure defence system that overlooked the Allies in many places (Picture 27). This was brought home to my great uncle Ernest Bailey of the 1st Essex with some impact when he was wounded in one of these unprotected trenches.

At the finish of the eight month campaign, mired in failure, the peninsula had to be evacuated, fortunately far more successfully than the initial landings. On the other hand, as well as the 250,000 allied losses it exacted an equally heavy price on Turkish forces, also costing them an estimated 250,000 men and producing consequent longer term effects in Palestine and the Middle East.

Overall, Gallipoli was a classic tragedy, a record of lost opportunity and eventual disaster. To the end of their days many a soldier who had been at Gallipoli regarded Winston Churchill with distaste, my grandparents included.

Time spent in reconnaissance is never wasted and it was clearly missing at Gallipoli. One positive thing was that those planning the later D-Day landings learned a great deal from the mistakes of Gallipoli thus enabling a successful invasion.

Finally, on evacuation, a parting remark from one soldier as they passed the graves of their fallen comrades, encapsulates the whole dreadful wasteful saga: "*I hope they don't hear us marching back to the beach.*" Amen.

NOTES

1. Captain (later Major) John Gillam of the (then) Army Service Corps kept a diary from the first day of the landings, 25th April 1915 at Cape Helles on W Beach, until the final evacuation of troops that took place in January 1916. The ACS was not a front line unit, being those who supplied vital equipment and popular with senior commanders for obvious reasons. As a result they usually lived under better conditions so became the butt of typical army humour earning disparaging nicknames, e.g. "Army Safety Corps". However, at Gallipoli they were right in the firing line throughout owing to the exposed and insecure nature of the British positions. Gillam's book is a detached and excellent account of the campaign and the men involved at the peninsula and Suvla Bay. As such it is a valuable primary source.

2. This was most likely my grandfather Frank, a Sergeant at the time, whose: "cheeriness and witticisms" are noted in the Essex Regiment Gazette (1937) on his retirement. Although not specifically attributed, I firmly believe he said it to relieve the tension for the men in his charge. That remark is typical of his brand of ironic humour which I remember when growing up and also is supported by one of his nieces.

3. Enfilading is fire directed from the flanks thus crisscrossing the advancing enemy. It is particularly effective when applied from a pronounced salient.

7.

The Somme

"**F**IX!" GOES the order. Bayonets that is. Crouched in their trenches on 1st July 1916 in the rising light of the dawn, with a residual covering of light mist, British soldiers prepare themselves to obey the order to go 'Over the Top' across 'No Man's Land' towards the German lines at The Somme. Even to this day, the words in that order and of the battle area still evoke a powerful reaction to the dreadful legacy of that most costly campaign.

The night before, thousands have moved silently along the trenches under cover of darkness. Sgt Richard Tawney of the Manchester Regiment observes that walking two miles in the restricted space of the communication trenches and in the dark with stoppages every ten or twenty yards is extremely disruptive and annoying. In some places, the trenches are so narrow along parts of this front (Picture 28), that congestion continually builds up and this trek takes an inordinate amount of time before the men are in position for tomorrow's battle. Few of them sleep other than fitfully, some not at all as they mentally face the battle to come.

Interestingly, Richard Tawney is actually an anti-war socialist but has enlisted from a sense of righteous outrage when Germany invaded neutral Belgium. In the battle, he survives being wounded and has to spend all of the first day pinned down by constant enemy sniper and machine gun fire in the bright sunlight beating down on no man's land. Eventually he is rescued by French stretcher bearers. After the war he becomes a leading socialist economist and reformer, one of the founders of the Welfare State and a leading proponent of adult education.

It is 07.15 hours. Zero hour approaches. It will be 07.30. The shattering booming of the heavy guns of the preliminary barrage has just stopped after

28. *A Somme Trench*

the constant week long barrage. Across the whole area there now emerges an eerie silence, a close stillness of the sort that comes before a thunder storm but interrupted by the faint clump of the last exploding shells in the far distance. Overnight there has been a slight rainfall. It is still moist but becoming drier as the sun begins to rise over the horizon.

Men in the trenches now wait apprehensively for the sound of their officers' bugles or whistles: the signal for action. Officers glance at their watches. There is extreme edginess as the attack has been already been postponed once. Is this really it? Is this the moment of truth? Reactions differ in an atmosphere of palpable tension. Smokers grab a last minute deep drag on yet another roll-up for habitual comfort. Many fiddle with water or their equipment. Some are momentarily caught in a reverie of family left behind or sneak a longing look at photos of wives and sweethearts. Others breathe deeply to try to calm themselves. Even the non-religious pray to be given strength for the task ahead. Those recruits completely new to combat are paralysed with fear. They find they literally cannot move at all.

It will pass when the action starts but right now their imaginations are rife with what will happen when they mount the ladders and face the enemy for the first time.

To a man, all are quiet as if locked in some trance. Butterflies swirl in stomach like the wait to start a race but no, this is much, much worse than that. Some throw their breakfast up at the last minute. Although it is only minutes the waiting seems interminable long, ironically described by one soldier as: "*agonising, like waiting for someone to die.*" The junior platoon and company officers, many only recently commissioned are themselves intensely scared but attempt to reassure their men by outwardly showing a controlled demeanour having hurriedly written last letters to their loved ones. In the 1st Bn Essex trench my grandfather Frank, promoted to RSM in the field at Gallipoli, keeps up morale along with other veteran NCOs steadying nerves, exhorting them to hold strong, stay in formation, follow all orders automatically and to concentrate on their objective.

Strangely enough, the greatest fear is not injury or death, both very likely in battle but letting down one's mates by failing in one's duty. Once the action starts they actually become fatalistic or: "*surprisingly more cool and matter of fact than in all my life*" as an Essex soldier describes it.

At 07.20 hours, 10 minutes before zero hour, a big mine is exploded at Hawthorn Redoubt in the Beaumont Hamel sector which signals the impending attack and this unfortunately propels the enemy into beating the British into this strategic hole left by that vast explosion.

At 07.30, ten minutes after the British have unaccountably failed to capitalise on any element of surprise, bugles and whistles sound and 120,000 men of the British Army, mainly hastily trained volunteers of General Rawlinson's Fourth Army, mount the stepladders and leave their trenches for what is confidently expected to be a slow controlled walk across the open fields. The prediction of the senior command officers is that this will be largely unopposed after a week's uninterrupted bombardment of enemy's front, including second and third line trenches and also their supply positions. This belief is viciously shattered by massive enemy machine gun fire. This is the beginning of The Battle of the Somme, which turns out to be many battles along several fronts in an offensive campaign that lasts five months.

The 1st Essex at Beaumont Hamel

One of the worst spots for devastating loss of life occurs in the northern sector of the general advance where 1st Essex and 1st Newfoundland Regiments, as part of 88th Brigade, are posted (Picture 29: Essex at lower left). On the first morning this is where these two regiments see fierce fighting in trying to achieve 29th Division's overall objective to capture the nearby tiny village of Beaumont Hamel which is strategically crucial as it gives the enemy a big visual advantage over the whole nearby landscape.

Although the village itself is in a small valley by the left of the River Ancre, there is a 135-foot high ridge behind it giving superb observational and military command over the British positions. This makes disguising the movements of the Division very difficult. This site is one of the most difficult to attack because the enemy is well protected by the chalk dug-outs and trees at their front which give them cover from the advancing troops.

Contemporary Picture 30 shows what kind of open ground faces the

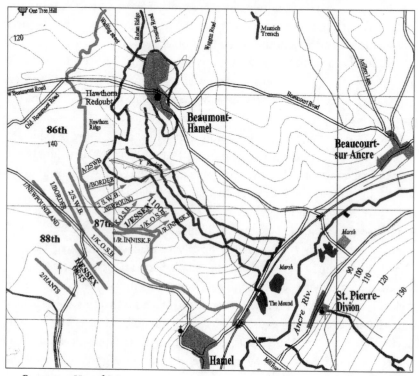

29. Beaumont Hamel Map

30. View from British trenches at Beaumont Hamel

soldiers as seen from their own trenches. Beaumont Hamel village and the German defences are behind those trees on the incline. Of course, on that morning, it is far removed from this calm greenery but is a picture of hell on earth with bullets and shells flying around spreading shrapnel and the whole area covered in swirling grey smoke. The enemy has five trench lines and the first two overlook the British attack area but any possible advantage has literally been blown by the many huge mine explosions along the lines, so the enemy is ready and waiting.

The Essex 1st, which has been in France since mid-March, on returning from Gallipoli via Eygpt, has 33 officers and nearly a thousand other ranks. They have initially been billeted at Louvencourt since 15th June and have since been incessantly training in offensive formations since arriving on this section of the front. A smart raid is conducted on the night of 26th June as a reconnaissance and this is accomplished without serious loss so confidence is high. The Battalion moves off from here under the command of Lt-Col Halahan, and forms up with 1st Newfoundland at the front between 21.00 and 03.30 hours on 30th June/1st July.

The order of battle is that 1st Essex has three companies in the front firing line with a company in reserve. The men for the first lines are accompanied by wire cutters and bridge carriers, whilst in the subsidiary lines there are Lewis gun carriers and grenadier squads for clearing the second and third line trenches. The idea is for support companies to leave the trenches when the first battalions have breached the crushed enemy wire. Unbeknown to them the week long allied bombardment has not achieved this objective and a massive slaughter is about to happen.

The 1st Essex is in position on the right ready to go over the top with the Newfoundlanders after the first units have achieved their targets. At this time both battalions are positioned about 300 yards behind the British front line and there is another equal distance of no man's land to be covered. However, confusion reigns in those initial attacks on this part of the front because the visual signals coming back from the observation posts are unclear and contradictory. Initially, the Essex advance is set for 10.00 hours but at 08.30 hours, Divisional HQ receives a report that the first-stage troops have taken the German front trench. Flares are up. Are they British or German? They look British so the first attack has succeeded. GOC de Lisle believes this so at 08.37 orders both the Essex and Newfoundland to advance there: "*as soon as possible*".

Communication lines between HQ and field commanders are also confused. The British Newfoundland commander, Lt-Col Hadow, is unclear about the telephoned order so asks if the trenches are actually captured. The reply is uncertain. Are they to move independently of the Essex? Yes, he must attack now. The latter regiment's war diary tells us: "*08.45 - Received orders on the telephone to move forward in conjunction with 1st Essex Regt and occupy the enemy's first trench ... and move as soon as possible. Asked Brigade if enemy's 1st trench has been taken and received reply to the effect that the situation was not cleared up. Asked Brigade if we were to move off to the attack independently of Essex Regt and received reply in the affirmative.*" This lack of clarity costs that battalion dearly.

It also keeps the Essex battalion waiting for a long time. It is the waiting before an attack that gets to the men more than anything else. We have the memory of one member of the 1st Bn, Private Charles Holman, MM, who many years later, recalls: "*We were waiting in lines for what felt like ages before we went forward. After that I'm afraid to say it's just a blur. You don't really remember much as soon as you come up the ladder and over the top – as the firing starts you just move as fast as you can.*"

The advance by these two regiments independently of each other is particularly disastrous to the Newfoundland. They should start their advance from the third (support) line but this is changed and the battalion is told to move up to the front line via the angled communication trenches, which link up support lines to the front. The increasing pile of dead bodies and wounded

31. 1st Newfoundlanders at 'St John's Road'

men from the earlier attacks are now clogging those communication trenches. There is smoke and noise everywhere. This causes a serious mobility problem for those still advancing.

At 09.15 hours, instead of trying to negotiate their way along the communication trenches, albeit very slowly, the inexperienced Newfoundlanders immediately leave the protection of their support trench in a sunken lane, dubbed St. John's Road (Picture 31, taken just beforehand) and clamber up into the open terrain. They have to travel 300 yards across exposed ground and immediately face a tornado of fire before they can even reach the British front line 'wire'. Those not already shot down within minutes are snagged in it at the mercy of the gunners' withering accuracy.

Meanwhile, the Essex battalion attempts to make its way through the communication trenches. This delay to the Essex means, that being the only group visible in no man's land, the Newfoundlanders are quickly sought out and mown down by machine gun fire over a half-mile range. Within 30 minutes this brave Dominion battalion has sustained 732 casualties (255 dead, 386 wounded, 91 missing) from its original 800 men. Every officer who has gone over the top is either wounded or dead. The carnage is indescribably final.

Now it is the turn of the 1st Essex. By the time they are in position the GOC Division has ordered a cessation of all attacks. However, due to the

32. The remains of Essex communication trench: attack towards the top right

numerous contact difficulties described, the message does not reach them. The tragedy has yet to play out in full for the Essex. In the communication trenches the Essex men are intermittently visible to the enemy overlooking them in the wooded area in front of the village and at Thiepval less than two miles down the road. With these communication trenches now completely blocked with bodies they are also eventually forced straight over the top but much nearer the objective. It is still to no avail. The two lead companies attempt to advance and suffer about 250 casualties before their CO calls a halt. Picture 32 shows the modern remains of that trench.

One Essex officer, Capt Paxton, notes: "*In my case, the front line trench was blocked and the company went over from the second line about 10.50am. We deployed in artillery formation, but at the same time I was told that our guns were shelling the German front line and ordered to hold up my attack. This was impossible, as I had launched the Company on its offensive.*" (Burrows: 208) RSM Bailey tries to organise things but cannot stem the increasing numbers of casualties amidst the increasing confusion and terror.

This attack on Beaumont Hamel fails from the very start for a number of reasons but one thing is certain though. It is not for the want of gallantry by the Essex and their fellow attackers in the face of ceaseless machine gun fire whilst exposed in the open, something acknowledged by the GOC 29th Division, Major-General de Lisle: "*Their bravery and the severity of the engagement are best evinced by the casualties, amounting to some 200 officers and 5,000 men.*" (Burrows: 209)

Subsequent to that attack on the first morning, de Lisle later acknowledges the impossibility of success against this impregnable position, established by the Germans, saying in his report: *"The sector allotted to the Division for attack had been converted by the enemy into a first class fortress, and it seems doubtful whether, if held by resolute men, it can be captured by frontal attack."*

Aftermath

After the dreadful day at Beaumont Hamel, on the following day, 1st Essex was relieved by the Gloucesters and went into a reserve position. General Hunter Weston inspected the battalion and some days later and it moved back to the front. They engaged in their habitual activity of clearing and cleaning up the front trenches and fortunately they were not under direct fire. Although their sector was quiet during this period of consolidation there was much incessant background rumbling from nearby Thiepval indicating there was fighting continuing in other sectors.

After this first phase of the battle, on 23rd July, the Brigade with 1st Essex marched to Beauval and caught a train for Poperinge, being billeted at Ypres Convent in Flanders. On 31st July, the 88th Bde started a now familiar task: that of improving the wire at the front line trenches. The Essex particularly utilised their obviously well honed digging skills in constructing a new line. During this period as an RSM Frank was engaged in the non-combatant side of the job: supervising digging and reconstruction, keeping up spirits and maintaining the discipline necessary to ensure that the men remained safe from possible enemy action as they remained exposed from the surrounding high ground of Thiepval Ridge.

On 9th August, the battalion relieved the Hants who the day before had been subjected to a nasty gas attack, with 215 casualties and, once again, the men from the county were improving trenches. Unsurprisingly, some wondered whether they had joined the Labour Corps (now Pioneers)! Two days on, some Germans attempted to bomb the front line but were repelled, this action sadly costing two Essex lives.

A week later, the battalion left the front line for rest and recuperation, returning to the front as part of the 12 day to 2-weeks rotation procedure on 29th August. There, they found the trenches flooded. A retaliatory gas attack was launched on the 31st and it travelled well in a fair wind. September started with pouring rain and on the 9th of the month the Essex was back into the Brigade's Reserve at Ypres, a name soon to be revived with another terrible significance.

For the remainder of The Somme campaign, the men of the 1st Battalion were variously involved: in mining attacks on the enemy, repairing breached barbed wire, back in reserve at Ypres Convent, in various sporting occasions where they conducted themselves with success, being inspected by the King of the Belgians and back at the front for further stints of action.

The battalion played a major role in the attack on Gueudecourt, just in front of Bapaume and Frank's Company were involved from the first, successfully taking the first line trenches. During the mopping up of the dug outs many Germans were killed and over 60 of the 6th Brandenburg Division, aka "*The Crown Prince's Little Berlin Boys*" were captured. On moving to the second line 15 Germans offered to surrender but then one attacked Lt Eastwood who shot him and other ranks shot the rest.

Finally, although overshadowed in the records by the gallant but inexperienced Newfoundland regiment and their staggering casualties, the 1st Essex too played a key part on this first day of the Somme offensive at the Beaumont Hamel sector, suffering 61 KIA and 155 wounded. Overall, 949 Essex Regiment men are commemorated at the impressive Thiepval Memorial (Picture 33).

BACKGROUND

The Somme offensive has a well-trodden and widely recognised position in

33. Thiepval Memorial

the British psyche so it is only necessary to revisit it here very briefly. It was initially planned as a combined allied campaign by the French and British C-in-Cs, Joseph Joffre and Douglas Haig, on a 20 mile front. It sought to put extra pressure on the Germans by relieving the Italians and Russians under attack on other fronts so they would have to reinforce their forces in the West.

Fourth Army General Rawlinson's tactical plan was to mount a short sharp attack known as 'bite and hold' and then gradually build upon that. However, owing to various military and larger political pressures, Haig insisted that this was too cautious. He wanted a bigger offensive with the remaining French on the south to be the knockout blow that would finally reopen the Western Front and bring an early end to the war.

Whilst still in the planning phase the Germans suddenly presented the allies with a serious threat elsewhere on the front by launching a massive attack on Verdun, a critical strategic transport junction which required the French to defend it at all costs. Consequently, eleven French divisions were diverted from the Somme which resulted in 130,000 less available men. It now became a predominantly British led offensive.

The underlying theory was to precede the ground offensive by the sheer force, volume and sustained duration of a heavy artillery bombardment that would soften up both the front and all back-up German defences, pulverising the occupants and leaving them dead or in disarray. Then the infantry would advance largely unopposed and occupy the first enemy trenches and onto the next lines. At this point, the cavalry would follow through by sweeping up the stragglers and the total result was that Germans would have been "*rolled up*". Haig also planned for a subsequent follow-up offensive move to Cambrai and onwards into Flanders sweeping up German reserves. In the event, save from the obvious obsolescence of cavalry, this part of the strategy did not occur until the end of the following year and even then was only partially successful.

First though, the artillery had to destroy the complex sequence of all the enemy trenches and the barbed wire defences that lay before them. The artillery bombardment started on 24th June, to precede a 29th June offensive but rain and mist delayed the ground attack so it carried on for an extra 48 hours. This bombardment was the largest ever to date in the history of warfare and could be heard in London, 180 miles away.

It involved a total of 1,500 artillery pieces, firing 1.7million shells by heavy guns, some of the heaviest being 12" naval guns mounted on railway carriage-bases and firing 1400lb shells over 12 miles, howitzers and 2" trench mortars

34. Shells in a Somme field

(known by the men as 'plum puddings'), which amounted to three shells per second both day and night. Even today French farmers are still ploughing up large numbers of shells (Picture 34) and many parts of the area are closed off to Battlefield tourists because of the danger of unexploded mines. This was the now second occasion that Frank was present at a great historical battle.

Defensive Advantage

Surely nobody could have survived this week long bombardment and be able to defend their trenches? Sadly, history has shown us that this expectation was a huge error. Once again, in British military history, unfounded confidence and ill-judged intelligence unfortunately outweighed the actuality to great cost.

Why? Simply, there were two reasons that weighed heavily against any success of the British offensive: strategic and geological. Firstly, the Germans won those positions in their original advance in 1914 and had two years worth of fortifications of deep dug-outs, various staged constructions of barbed wire and other defensive obstacles. They had obviously selected the highest and most prominent features wherever possible from which they oversaw the surrounding low land and also the allied positions. (Two years later during the final 100-day allied push in 1918, when British soldiers overran the German trenches, they were horrified to discover they had been overlooked by the enemy for most of that time).

Secondly, the undulating land of the Somme Valley is largely comprised of exceptionally compacted chalk which made it relatively easy to construct tunnels and deep dugouts. The Germans had constructed a series of subterranean forts, some at least 30 feet deep, especially in and around the small village of Beaumont Hamel, to which they retired during the heavy bombardment. Although it was utterly unbearable enduring the deafening and maddening noise above ground they were virtually safe underground although they did suffer some devastating collapses. Also, unfortunately for the advancing British, the massive artillery bombardment failed to completely destroy any of the barbed wire, which was one of its main objectives. Not only that, but more seriously, the Germans had three tiers of protective barbed wire spread out all along their lines, most of it intact.

The artillery offensive had been largely ineffective. Many of the shells fired were shrapnel and the rushed inferior technology meant 30% or more proved to be 'duds' by failing to explode. Those that did so produced much less than the expected damage. Additionally, many more failed to hit their targets owing to the inaccuracy of the gunners. Therefore, on the morning of the attack, the scene was already set for a huge disaster. The troops, many of them recent recruits, were ordered to walk from their trenches towards those of the enemy. Why walk? Why not run or even crawl across and stay out of sight?

To us today, this sounds absolutely crazy: walking across a large cratered field with the possibility of being mown down. The answer mainly lies in what weight the men had to carry across that expanse. Each man was weighed down with 70lbs of equipment, about half his weight, which included two days rations in a haversack, a Lee Enfield rifle and long bayonet. He carried 250 rounds of ammunition with two Mills Bombs and two sandbags. Some rifles had wire cutters attached to the end of their barrels.

The distances to be covered to reach the first enemy trenches varied greatly along the British front. No man's land was anything between a few yards, a quarter of a mile to a mile and in some places this was on an uphill incline. For instance, some men, in the north near Albert, had to cover 900 yards in the open to their first target and then, having captured it, go on again a further 1000 yards to the second trench.

Not much imagination is required to see that running a long way with all this would be very exhausting and impractical. As to crawling, because of the supporting artillery fire, the troops would have been susceptible to being hit by their own shells if they spent too much time in open ground. Ironically, on this morning, the quicker they reached the enemy's front line the safer they were. Logically then the walk was the chosen option. Officers were dressed the same as other ranks to avoid being specifically picked off and create uncertainty or even chaos in the Germans when under fire. In the event it did not stop 8 out of 10 from one brigade being hit.

In some sectors, the men emerged initially to an unlikely and unsettling silence at first. They began to cross the empty land on the now hot sunny dawn with fixed bayonets and 'in close order'. They thought the artillery had done its job and were initially relieved. As they approached their first objective, the barbed wire, they found to their horror it was still largely untouched by the massive bombardment. Not only that, but their wire cutters could not cut through the German wire. There they were stuck and standing crucially exposed to possible fire on open ground and unable to advance any further. Then, suddenly, the deadly crackling of machine gun fire erupted cutting a swathe through the advancing troops and men began to fall as they were mercilessly scythed to shreds.

Bodies were strewn everywhere and cries of pain rent the noisy air. Successive battalions of different regiments failed even to reach the still intact wire being decimated well before that whilst those that did were impaled on it. Contrary to the senior commanders' expectations, the enemy had not been routed by the bombardment: quite the reverse. Machine gunners abounded in numbers and were very well placed to repel the advancing troops. The German defenders, protected deep underground in their network of tunnels and dug-outs (Stöllen) had emerged, albeit shakily and were quickly ensconced in their well-prepared defensive posts and engaged in what has since been ominously described as a turkey shoot. One British soldier compared the bullets and shrapnel flying around with large hailstones whilst a German defender later stated: "*If only they had run they'd have overwhelmed us.*"

By the afternoon of that hot July day, under clear pale blue skies, over

19,000 men lay dead in no man's land. Subsequently, it was discovered that 35,000 men died in those unprotected fields from wounds that could easily have been treated if they had received attention in time. The casualties were horrendous, especially on the first day when 60% British Army officers were killed. Overall, British losses that day were 57,400 plus men with very little strategic advantage gained. In contrast, the French achieved their objective and suffered losses of a few thousand. (This is a comparable repeat of the fate of the two armies in the Crimea.)

The Somme Offensive was the largest and bloodiest for the British Army lasting from 1st July until it petered out in November. A total of about 420,000 British and Empire troops, 200,000 French and 500,000 to 650,000 German lives were lost (exact figures vary). In the overall war effort this offensive cost over 1.25 million lives, virtually removing an entire irreplaceable generation of young men and it gained very little real strategic advantage for either side. Although popularly known by this single name, what we call The Somme was really a series of interlinked engagements along a very long front in a very drawn out campaign. The British sector stretched from Serre in the north diagonally to Maricourt in the south. By the end of it all the deepest advance into enemy territory was generally agreed to be about five miles.

Much has been said about the troops walking into enemy fire and, as seen, one reason was because of the amount of heavy equipment to be carried across no man's land.

It is important to record though that there was another consideration. The army had lost most of its veteran professionals during 1914-15 and, by 1916 its ranks were predominately made up of Kitchener's New Army. Most of these young volunteers were untested in real battle. In the planning stage, Rawlinson and Haig worried that these inexperienced soldiers would be unable to adapt to rapidly changing conditions and think under pressure like any battle hardened veteran. They would naturally dive for cover at the first volley and this would be disastrous in the first attack because it would disrupt discipline under fire and cause disarray to the coherence requited for tactical success. Therefore, these men were consistently drilled and discipline was rigorously applied to counter any resistant tendencies.

In a sad twist of fate, the loss of life was exacerbated by a small piece of equipment actually designed to save men's lives while they crossed no man's land and entered enemy positions. It was a small tin triangle attached on the soldier's back to glint in the daylight so the artillery spotters and the RFC could easily discern their own forces. Glint it did with every movement in the bright sunshine of that day enabling the German machine gunners to more easily achieve greater accuracy and thus increase the death toll.

Despite this awesome failure the campaign did finally propel the slow learning curve of the British Army into overdrive that quickly translated into a new type of technical training. As opposed to the Germans who concentrated upon field skills, viz. initiation of storm troopers, British troops advanced in an integrated 'all arms' formation with a simultaneous artillery 'creeping barrage' (artillery laying down fire some yards ahead of advancing infantry to disable an enemy response), cavalry, along with tanks and air cover. Also, they applied smaller groups in attack covering each other with fire in movement. In 1917, the fruits of this combined operations approach were felt to better effect from Arras to Cambrai.

According to many informed military and historical authors, the C-in-C, General Sir Douglas Haig has to take the overall blame for the massive and senseless slaughter that characterised The Somme. Not for planning and pushing the offensive beyond Rawlinson's original limited objectives but because he stubbornly resisted any adaptation to the prevailing conditions. He continually ordered Rawlinson to send men over the top into withering enemy fire even after it was clearly obvious it would not achieve any significant result. Whenever the weather was appropriate he ordered further attacks again and again.

It is that behaviour that led to the unverified description of brave men and obstinate generals as *"lions led by donkeys"*. In that evaluation, many regard Haig as a key member of the latter. In recent years, there has been a considerable revision of that consensus view about the role of Haig. I am no military historian by any means but my lay reading of the campaign has slightly tempered that view.

To redress the balance it is worth noting that, despite the massive loss of life, the Battle of The Somme did nevertheless achieve certain positive results. It seized the initiative from the Germans for the first time on the Western Front and necessitated the withdrawal of about 600,000 of their men away from beleaguered Verdun, eventually forcing them to abandon their attack on that city. The pool of German manpower was more limited than the allies and this bloody offensive stretched it to the limit, particularly killing off many experienced officers and NCOs which they could ill afford to lose. The British by contrast were largely inexperienced soldiers but those who did survive this hellish conflict gained invaluable military experience which paid off by providing a springboard for the continuous series of battles in the following year.

As an ex-cavalry officer, Haig did champion Britain's new secret weapon: the tank. This made its world debut on 15th September 1916 at Flers de Courcelette and he was also responsible for the later and final successful campaigns in 1917-18. Finally, on that bright morning bayonets may have been 'fixed' but the trench war was far from fixed.

8.

From Arras to Cambrai

THE THIRD year of the war was very significant for Sergeant Major Frank Bailey as he was both gassed in Belgium and later awarded a medal for gallantry in France. The 1st Battalion found itself fully involved in a series of interlinked battles in 1917 ranging from the various actions around Arras, particularly a desperate attack and defence at the small but strategically placed village of Monchy-le-Preux, and carrying on north to the Belgian front for engagements at Ypres, Langemarck, Passchendaele and then back to France for the famous tank deployment at Cambrai. The maps (Pictures 35, 38, 39) show the relative places and movements.

The Essex at Monchy

For their part on the 1st April the Essex march from Flesselles to Beauval, then cover a further twenty mile slog arriving outside Arras just after the capture of Monchy on 12th April. During this time RSM Frank Bailey is mentioned in dispatches by General Haig on 9th April (*Frank's War and Peace*). The previously planned French attack in the north is delayed by bad weather necessitating Haig to keep up the pressure at Arras. A further break-out advance is planned pushing eastwards from outside Monchy.

At dawn on 14th April, again linked by fate, 1st Essex, under Lt-Col Halahan and 1st Newfoundland, under Lt-Col Forbes-Robertson, are ready east of Monchy on the apex of the British salient to gain control of Infantry Hill flanked by two woods: Bois du Sart (Picture 35: right) and Bois du Vert (Picture 35).

At 05.30 hours, the two battalions start the attack and take the hill defended by the 17th, 18th and 23rd Bavarian Regiments. It is on a narrow front of no more than 1,000 yards and as obvious from the map no reserve protection on either flank. The battalion commanders worry that the salient will be increased too much thereby inviting a counterattack. The battalion on the right is instructed to take Bois du Vert if vacated by the enemy to start a constructive protection of that flank.

The advance is under 'creeping barrage' which requires efficient communications, split-second timing and, above all, immediate compensation for the inevitably deteriorating accuracy. Now improved, doubtless better application would have saved many lives at Beaumont Hamel the year before.

By 06.30 1st Essex report Z, Y, and W Companies have reached their target on Infantry Hill and are digging in (the Essex are very good at this!) but also that there are large numbers of Germans about. Capt Foster's X Company, with RSM Bailey accompanying, immediately come under intense heavy machine gun fire at Arrowhead Copse but assails it with great courage and establishes strong points in Twin Copses (Picture 35: right). The Bavarians have been experimenting with 'elastic defence' that involves having only one Rifle Company positioned in the front trench. After the initial attack this unit contrives a phoney retreat thus creating a passage through which

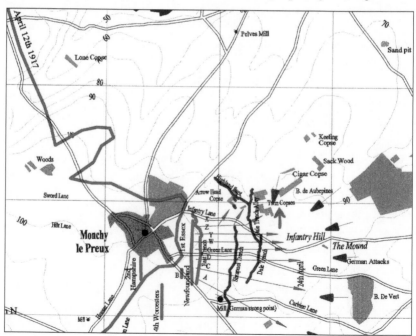

35. *X Company, 1st Battalion Essex position at Monchy-le-Preux (upwards arrow)*

the advancing troops travel. Thus this forms a deeper salient whereupon a counterattack occurs on the three exposed sides of the apex with devastating results.

However, the good news is that the 3rd Bavarian Division, a recognised crack unit, inexplicably fails to employ this elastic defence today. The Essex W Company Captain is wounded and is carried back to HQ where he reports a large concentration of Germans in Bois du Sart (Picture 35: big grey patch on right). Coincidentally they are preparing for their own attack on Monchy. With telephone lines cut, HQ cannot risk an artillery attack on the wood. Consequently, the action of the first Essex companies coincides with this German attack so they run straight into a large force, being overwhelmed with disastrous losses.

In his report of 11th May, 88th Brigade CO Brigadier-General Cayley supports this, as follows: "*The Brigadier wishes to place on record his appreciation of the gallant work done by the 88th Brigade in the hard fighting of 14th April. The attack carried by the 1st Essex and the 1st NFLD was entirely successful, the objectives being brilliantly gained. It seems certain that the enemy had planned an attack in force on Monchy on the morning of the 14th. This attack fell on two battalions which had advanced and though they were nearly destroyed in doing so, they appear to have completely broken up and disorganised the German attack. The hostile troops consisted of a fresh Bavarian Division which had not been in the previous fighting.*" (War Diary, 88th Infantry Brigade)

This shows that these enemy troops have only been deployed there recently strongly suggesting they are transfers from the Eastern Front where Russia is beginning to collapse. Nevertheless, the Essex defend the position vigorously and although largely destroyed have broken the 3rd Bavarian offensive. A few X Company survivors appear and are quickly organised in defence by the Adjutant, Lt Lawson with RSM Bailey.

Along with help from the Hants and Worcester units, Monchy is held however. The battalion diary notes: "*No further news could be gathered as to the fate of this company. A few men eventually rejoined the battalion and from their statements it is certain that all platoons reached their proper positions, where they were at once attacked by very superior German forces and were finally overwhelmed in these positions at a time between 6.30 am and 7.30am.*" (War Diary, 1st Essex Regiment)

At 10.00, a wounded Essex man appears at Lt-Col Forbes-Robertson's repositioned 1st Newfoundland HQ, in the centre of Monchy, and reports news that all his battalion are either killed or captured. Subsequently, it appears that the Germans have mounted a devastating attack at 07.30 hours and during this action the 1st Essex are 'rolled up' and the enemy carry on to destroy the Newfoundlanders as well.

Aftermath

The 1st Essex started out this action with 30 officers and 892 men but these were reduced by 17 and 644 respectively: killed, wounded or missing at the end of the day (Burrows). The majority of Essex men who died there on Infantry Hill are most likely still there because this spot was fought over again and again for months thereafter. It was at this point that the remnants of 1st Essex and Newfoundland battalions were necessarily and temporarily combined into a composite "*1st Newfoundessex*" battalion with a total strength of 400 men.

A critical account is given by a 29th Divisional Staff Officer: "*The attack east of Monchy on the 14th was but one more example of the futility of piecemeal attacks beloved of the Higher Command and abhorred by the Divisions and still more by the Brigades and Battalions. Had our attack east of Monchy been part of a general attack we should not in all probability have lost two battalions and might moreover gained and held our objective. [...] As a result, when the Germans counterattacked, there was practically nobody in our front line at Monchy and it was only the courage and presence of mind of Forbes-Robertson that saved the situation.*"(Fox, 2000)

After the last ditch defence at Monchy the battalion moved back at Arras on 11th May only to find the trenches they had dug waterlogged making them difficult to defend. They then were posted into reserve on 21st May just after a very heavy artillery barrage that killed many men and continued in and out of the front until 30th when there was a huge thunderstorm which completely flooded the recently dried out trenches. Unbeknown to them this was the forerunner of the continual rainfall that would later turn the Flanders front into a mud sea.

June peacefully passed with trench duties, saying goodbye to Arras and moving back to Montrelet, north of Amiens, for 20 days simulated attack training this being aimed at the forthcoming offensives in Flanders which would become known to history as 3rd Ypres, or more notoriously as Passchendaele. The 1st Bn relieved the Grenadier Guards at the front on 21st July and it is while they were engaged in preparations to breach the Yser Canal they first experienced mustard gas. The Germans started employing the new deadlier and longer lasting mustard gas in the Langemarck-Poelkappelle area in April 1917.

The Essex achieve their Langemarck

This particular attack is a highly trained integrated combination of artillery and RFC support. At 04.45 hours on 16th August 1st Essex are lined up ready having ploughed their way through knee deep mud on the roads to the attack point. At the beginning of this action many men have to be dragged out of the mud immediately because being sucked under is most likely fatal in its consequences. This essential diversion delays the attack time. By 07.45 the Essex men achieve their objective having gone diagonally across over 700 yards of open ground with X Company managing to take out the deadly snipers and later taking 80 prisoners.

That this prior training had worked is acknowledged by the Brigade CO: "*The utmost determination was needed by all ranks to get through the mud and swamps, and this was shown in the highest degree. The most satisfactory feature of the day's operations was the manner in which the lessons taught in training were applied by all ranks without any hesitation and with the highest intelligence.*"

The Essex CO also praises his men: "*The whole terrain was a mass of water-filled shell holes, and the effort to cross it entailed supreme determination by our men. One cannot speak too highly of the spirit and gallantry of all ranks, whilst the way in which successive strong points were tackled and covering fire to all flanks was afforded reflects the greatest credit on both the officers who trained them and the men who carried out the operation.*"

Both these quotes from Burrows (1931), and other commendations of the Essex and their counterparts the Hants on their performance in this action, clearly show that the army has learned from The Somme experience. It has reached a new plateau which will act to launch more success in the months to come.

Between 19th and 23rd August, the Essex men are back in the Langemarck area and Frank's company (200 plus men) are holed up on the British side of a captured half-made pillbox. The battalion is continuously under heavy shelling losing seven killed and 23 wounded. Perhaps this pillbox incident is the one my grandmother confused with the DCM action at Cambrai? However, there is no firm evidence of the capture of German prisoners in this pillbox.

Aftermath

Throughout September, 1st Essex were involved in a further intensive training regime in preparation for the forthcoming Battle of Cambrai. This training was only relieved on the 18th by an open-to-all-units drumming competition and the "Drums of the 44th" won the premier award. The prize was spent

36. Drum Major Ernest Bailey

on a silver model of an Essex drummer in full fighting kit, with steel helmet, and this was later displayed in the Officer's Mess. The winners then gave a special performance to the COs of the 5th Army and 29th Division. The army commander congratulated the Sgt Drummers, of whom one was Frank's brother Ernest Bailey (Picture 36).

On 26th September Frank received a nasty birthday present: he was gassed but: *"remained at duty"*. Mercifully it sounds as if it was not mustard gas as any injuries were not so serious to prevent him from remaining at the front.

Although the French used tear gas in 1914, it was the Germans who first researched, developed and applied poison gases on an industrial scale. They used tear gas against the Russians on the Eastern Front in January 1915 but it froze. However, this was soon followed by a chlorine attack at 2nd Ypres in April 1915. The British responded in kind during September at Loos and as the war progressed the Germans employed more increasingly deadly gases, the most threatening being mustard gas. The effects of mustard gas were varied and many long term, varying from hours to weeks. In some cases, secondary problems appeared years later, particularly affecting the respiratory and immune system.

Masnières for Cambrai

Like many in the 29th Division, the 1st Bn has spent three days non-stop getting to the attack area. They form up at 06.30 and by 08.45 are ready and advance to the sound of bugles at 11.00, moving behind four tanks in a diamond formation. Frank and his company are right in the vanguard of this formation as it moves forward and they take many prisoners.

The immediate objective is the bridge at Masnières to allow an advance into Cambrai. By 13.00, 1st Bn reach the St. Quentin Canal. It is imperative that they reach the other side. The Germans have unsuccessfully tried to demolish the stone and iron bridge to halt the advance. Although the bridge is obviously weakened the decision is nevertheless taken to send a tank over

37. 'Flying Fox' on collapsed bridge at Masnières

it. However, when *"Flying Fox"* crosses it, the bridge collapses in slow motion as observed by those present and ironically the tank which is to spearhead the attack is marooned across the canal blocking the way forward for the infantry (Picture 37, above).

This disastrous start is compounded by some accurate sniper fire that prevents any further attempts to cross the bridge. After dark, a small detachment of the Essex cross the canal and clear out all the troublesome snipers that have been pinning them down and at 03.00 the Masnières-Cambrai Road is clear. After the initial impetus, the attack stalls and with many of the tanks now out of operation through mechanical failure, the overall advantage is eventually lost.

The initial success of the battle results in the church bells being rung at home on 21st November for the first time since the start of the war to celebrate a real major breakthrough on the Western Front.

On the 24th there is such heavy German shelling on the recently gained British positions that the whole battalion is moved into a large dug out. Like the Somme, the chalky soil has allowed the Germans to construct these with entrances in the streets so this decision saves many lives. Another heavy bombardment on 29th November includes many gas shells.

The inevitable counterattack comes at 08.30 hours on 30th November with 20 divisions (about 300,000 men) and they introduce their own new secret weapon: stormtroopers. The attack is so rapid that most of the British 'standing to' are quickly overwhelmed. The land lost by the Germans is quickly won back and both sides regress into their trenches. A desperate rearguard action is fought by 29th Division between 1st-5th December, resisting by day and retiring by night.

Aftermath

This whole defensive action was against great odds but the casualties were 42,000 with roughly the same for the Germans. The 1st Essex lost 103 officers and other ranks in the area of Masnières. The battalion cleaned and rested up on 7th December and then started more training the next day. On 18th December they moved off but had to travel by road in deep snow drifts.

It was during this battle that RSM Frank Bailey conducted himself with valour in a tight situation and was awarded the DCM, the then highest award for NCOs. Once again he was directly involved in a life or death situation but somehow managed to turn it to advantage and help his comrades get out of it (*Frank's War and Peace*).

Coincidentally, the utterly exhausted Essex men left the front as Russia and Germany declared an armistice. An observer noticed that they *"reeled and stumbled rather than marched."*

On Christmas Day 1917, the men from Essex tucked into a most welcome dinner of roast pork and Christmas pudding and General Hunter Weston called in on them to visit the few regimental veteran survivors who had served with him at Gallipoli.

BACKGROUND

After their horrendous losses on the Somme, the Germans had taken stock and decided on a new strategy. In February 1917 they covertly retired to a recently constructed system of formidable interlocking defences known by the British as the Hindenburg Line. This was the northern section of a much longer line of defensive emplacements from Lille in the north to St Quentin in the south. It was one mile deep in three lines, with barbed wire in 50 foot zigzag formations, along with concrete tunnels and artillery hidden on reverse slopes invisible to advancing troops. During this withdrawal, they instigated a scorched earth policy destroying all equipment, poisoning the wells, setting souvenir booby traps and leaving small companies in the villages to harass and delay allied advances.

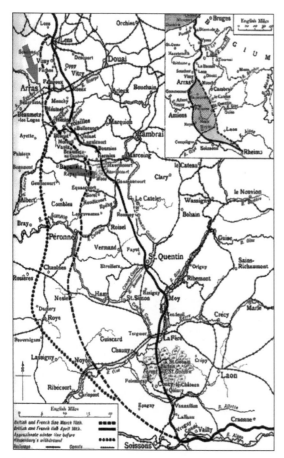

38. *Arras main map*

There were necessary advantages for the Germans in this strategy. They had straightened out the salient between Arras and Bapaume (Picture 38, between arrows), ironically giving up the few desperately fought over miles east of Beaumont Hamel. The result was their line was now more densely and easily defended requiring fewer men thus enabling the redeployment of 130,000 men. Obviously, this defensive position would be much more difficult to overrun successfully.

French General Nivelle was keen to attack the enemy in the northern sector of the Aisne, with 1.2 million French troops using the recently developed creeping barrage tactic. The role of the British was to create a diversionary attack around Arras that would to pull enemy troops away from the French attack and allow the French to break through with both armies linking up at Cambrai. However, the offensive failed and ended in disaster. It was based on false intelligence about German positions, now since altered by their withdrawal to the Hindenburg Line, and secrecy of the allied plans was seriously compromised both by Nivelle talking it up to all and sundry and then the plans falling into enemy hands.

The casualties were enormous and the French soldiers finally mutinied against their commanders with serious consequences for their front line. Fortunately, the Germans never got to hear about this weakness for that would have been doubly disastrous. By March, this offensive became more

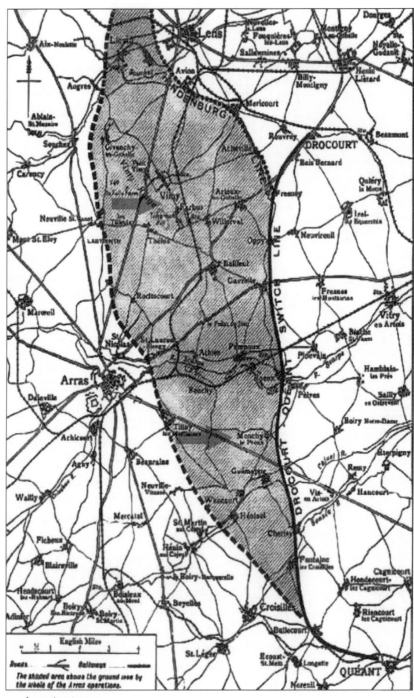

39. *Arras inset map*

strategically crucial to the allies as the Russian war effort began to collapse and the Germans started to pour in extra troops to the Western Front.

Arras

The Arras offensive started on a snowy Easter Sunday, 9th April, along a 15-mile front and, although costly, was initially successful. Unfortunately, unexpected winter weather had set in and this severely hampered all activity. The Canadian Corps' objective was to take strategically vital Vimy Ridge (Picture 39, upper arrow) a highly fortified position. They succeeded spectacularly using a meticulously planned integrated attack and had taken it within three days and, without adequate cover, the Germans withdrew.

Arras was crucial to final allied success and yet in comparison to The Somme historians tend to neglect it. This is unjustified as the shaded area on the enlarged inset map (Picture 39) shows the considerable territorial gains made in the offensive which officially concluded on 15th May.

Like The Somme before it, Arras comprised several ongoing phased actions at various points on the front. As a vital part of this campaign it was also very important to take the small village of Monchy-le-Preux (Picture 39, lower arrow) about 200 feet above the River Scarpe with a commanding view over the surrounding low lying land which had been held by Germans since 1914. This continuous pressure on the German lines was intended to give them no rest in the hope that a full breakthrough could finally be achieved in Flanders.

Third Ypres (Passchendaele)

Haig wanted the BEF to break out of the Ypres Salient in Flanders, so after a massive bombardment from 18th July, a ground attack began on 31st July with the goal of smashing through and swinging north to the Belgian ports of Ostende and Zebrugge. The overall goal was to destroy the U Boat docks thus preventing further attacks on Allied shipping.

The heavens opened on 2nd August and the already shell-cratered battlefield became an impossible and very dangerous quagmire of glutinous mud. The attack was stalled for ten days and the subsequent battles lasting over three months resulted in massive 'Somme-like' losses for little advantage. Unlike the Somme though this was not chalky terra firma but rather the battlefield was sitting on reclaimed marshland which rainfall quickly transformed into a swamp. Consequently, it was impossible to dig adequate trenches, owing to the ever-present water and mud. Mostly, the cover for the troops comprised shallow dugouts augmented by sandbags and pillboxes. The real problem was that when it rained, which it did continuously, these defences completely collapsed and became untenable.

This glutinous mud now became an even greater danger than enemy fire because it could suck a man or even an entire gun team under in seconds. Fear of the elements reigned. If anyone failed to stay on the duckboards spread out across the dreadful grey landscape, then that was it. Wounded men drowned in the mud and at night working details went out never to be seen again. Battle hardened soldiers who had been at the Somme said it had been a picnic compared to this!

Huge rats infested the shallow trenches and dug outs, feeding off the dead bodies which were everywhere and nowhere more startling than at the end of a spade when trying to re-dig some defence. Visually, the troops were continuously reminded of their plight during the day by the sight of the dead and wounded snagged in the thick barbed wire. The smell of the rotting flesh of dead men and horses permeated everywhere. The cries and screams for help by the wounded in no man's land were a constant reminder of the deadly sniper threat. To add to the problems, as the campaign progressed it became bitingly cold.

The menu of death in the area of Ypres/Passchendaele was now increased by the development of more advanced weapons of industrialised warfare. There was now dreaded mustard gas which burnt terribly but also had a hidden threat. It lingered latently on clothing and in the trenches. A few tiny splatters undetected on a uniform in the cold outside would be harmless but these would immediately be triggered by any warmth, setting off the gas and attacking everyone nearby. The man had to exit immediately to save his colleagues.

Apart from the danger from slow drowning and burning gas, there was also the threat of gangrene for unattended wounds, entombment in collapsing dugouts, flamethrowers and flaming oil bombs. It is nothing short of amazing that any man kept going at all in these conditions let alone engaging in conflict. In fact the men consistently struggled just to perform mundane daily functions within this environment. It was indeed hell on earth.

Along with the Somme the name of this small Belgian village has since assumed the symbolic mantle of the futility of massive death and destruction but with added mud. The famous iconic photo of soldiers on duckboards at Chateau Wood (Picture 40) portrays a scene from an alien but earthly hell.

40. *Duckboards at Chateau Wood, Passchendaele (iwm: E (AUS) 1220)*

Tanks at Cambrai

The battle for the control of Cambrai started on the morning of 20th November 1917. The Cambrai front was a crucial point in the whole area having a railhead that led directly to Germany and being positioned at a vital transport junction. This time the German front was probed without any lengthy advance artillery bombardment to warn the enemy but a quick intensive battery simultaneously combined with infantry and air support and the special surprise ingredient of massed ranks of the new mobile weapon: over 400 tanks (Picture 41, next page).

The preparation for his battle was very thorough, careful and intensely secretive. Camouflage screens were erected behind the lines to hide movements likely to interest the enemy observers and all tracks made were immediately covered up with loose dirt to avoid the attention of enemy air reconnaissance. Men and equipment had been moved to the front very quietly at night and rested during the day. To avoid alerting the enemy the tanks had tortuously travelled at their slowest possible speed so as not to send

41. *Tanks at Cambrai (iwm: Q 5572)*

underground tremors.

The spearhead targets for 29th Division were the canal bridges at Marcong and Masnières which were vital to the success and 1st Essex was detailed for this tough job because of their Gallipoli experience.

The OC Tank Corps, young Brigadier-General Elles, had been waiting impatiently for this day. Despite forbidding his commanders to go in the vanguard he nevertheless decided to lead the tank charge in his own machine called "*Hilda*". Zero hour was the hour before sunrise. It had been a bitterly cold night so the ground was relatively dry and the whole division felt much roused after its allocation of rum before the 'off'. A bugle sounded and a gun fired to alert all along the line. Over 1,000 artillery pieces opened up with a massively deafening and unusually accurate barrage that shook the earth all around but destroyed all the German batteries.

The Germans, who had become well accustomed to the longer 'registered' (trial and error) bombardments ahead of an attack, were completely taken by surprise by this new intensive much shorter battery. Immediately it finished, advancing troops moved forward in a fully integrated attack. Now there was a second surprise for the enemy.

He could not believe his eyes because there was "*Hilda*" bearing down on his front. It was not the tank itself because the Germans had seen them in limited numbers before and not very successfully at Flers-Courcelette in the Somme. No, it was the fact that there were so many of them all inexorably moving towards the German lines with attached fascine rods (bound cylindrical bundles of brushwood to bolster passage in undulating ground), various items of grappling material and some which had attached wire-cutters to combat German barbed wire.

The German defences were threefold. First the Hindenburg Line and then a support line about a mile and half behind it with the reserve around Marcong and Masnières between three and four miles further back. The Hindenburg Line, considered to be impenetrable was breached by five to six miles. However, the tanks were cumbersome and slow and could only traverse the ground at about 4mph, many becoming bogged down in the now thawing earth and getting caught in various wide ditches on either side of the lanes acting as tank traps. By the later 'Blitzkrieg' standards this was a very pedestrian advance.

One advantage to Cambrai was that it introduced new technology and tactics to the battlefront and held out the carrot of a return to pre-1914 mobile campaigning. The British dovetailed their attacking formations by seriously developing their artillery batteries in a devastating fashion by rapid intensive fire with increased accuracy, combined and coordinated with simultaneous infantry, mechanised and air-support. Meanwhile the Germans started to use small scale troop movements and elastic defensive tactics effectively. The latter proved to be successful in that they confused the enemy by suddenly changeable tactics and enabled small units to pass through and behind the front lines under cover more easily.

The devastating effects of the German counterattack, with their numbers continually bolstered by divisions from the now collapsed Russian front, caused the British to fight a desperate rearguard action to hang onto their gains. The "*Incomparable 29th*" managed to hang on: just.

1918 Reorganisation

After Cambrai, 1st Essex was part of the reduction of brigades from four to three battalions. This occurred on 1st February when they were transferred to 37th Division. Everyone, from all ranks, was sad because the battalion had been in the 29th Division since being formed in 1914 and active at Gallipoli, Beaumont-Hamel in the Somme, Arras, Monchy-le-Preux, Ypres and Cambrai. The Divisional CO wrote to the battalion Colonel expressing: "*regret at being deprived of the services of a fine battalion.*" They included RSM Frank Bailey, DCM and Sgt Drummer Ernest Bailey who had been with them all that time and through the hell of those battles.

On the day they left many COs of other regiments came to say goodbye. Burrows says that the scene was: "*a fit subject for artist, and perhaps, one day, when the people of Essex desire to have painted some of the great incidents of the war in which county units were concerned, the farewell of the 1st Essex to the 88th Brigade and the 29th Division at Vlamertinghe will find a place.*" One can only hope but perhaps it would be better if they had a specific memorial at Beaumont Hamel.

9.

Battlefields

W HILST WRITING this book, I felt it important to try capturing some feel for the places where grandad Frank, great uncle Ernest and their 1st Essex comrades fought their battles: Gallipoli, Beaumont Hamel, Monchy-le-Preux, Ypres, Langemarck, Cambrai and Passchendaele. Although not with the Essex, recently discovered brother Edgar also fought but died of wounds sustained in Flanders near Ypres. Apart from Cape Helles, Ann and I visited these Western Front battlefields to experience them first hand and pay our due respects.

42. W Beach Gallipoli today

For those like me interested in following in the footsteps of their forbears or just to visit out of interest there are many books available that both give detailed accounts of these battles and a guide to these many memorials. They are well worth consulting before you embarking on your trip.

Cape Helles, Gallipoli

In the course of this search, I gained considerable knowledge about the first-day landings of 1st Battalion Essex on the Cape on 25th April 1915. They landed on W Beach (Picture 42, today, previous page), to reinforce the 1st Lancashire Fusiliers. Although it belies belief now, on that morning this beach was probably the most suitable of them all for such a landing but, as is blatantly obvious, this simultaneously left them very exposed. Of course it looks like a nice spot for a beach picnic today but obviously at the time it very was far from it. The men from Essex managed to secure a position for their headquarters by nightfall (*Gallipoli*).

They survived there for a very long time dug into the hills overlooking the beach but in conditions that were nothing short of dreadful. One soldier arriving a month later noted that the hills, as seen from the sea, looked like a beehive with all the dug outs and the soldiers like ants milling around following their allotted tasks.

Despite the 1981 film of the same name, Gallipoli is the graveyard of many more British, French and Colonial troops than those from Australia, much to their surprise. The ANZAC landing has entered mythology but despite its deservedness, it needs redressing and balancing in the bigger picture.

There are many memorials from both sides of the conflict on the peninsula so anyone looking for a relative's name needs to pinpoint it with the Commonwealth War Graves Commission (CGWC) before arriving to avoid the proverbial 'looking for a needle in a haystack'. There is a British and Commonwealth Memorial at Cape Helles which lists those from 1st Essex who died there (Holt & Holt, 2000).

At some points the allied troops and Turkish defenders were little more than a few yards apart thus making life very tenuous. Anyone looking over the parapet inevitably lost their head by sniper fire, hence the man shown looking through a homemade periscope (Picture 43).

Beaumont Hamel

The present day site of this French battlefield, on D4151, off D50 from Albert or D919 from Arras, is now the Newfoundland Memorial and the most

43. British periscope in a Gallipoli Trench

visited of the sites, attracting about 125,000 people a year. As we entered, we were struck with how serene it was and a very light drizzle permeated the pale early morning sunlight through the fir trees lending the whole experience an eerie stillness. Wandering around the trenches it was as if the power of those

44. Beaumont Hamel 2008

45. Beaumont Hamel 1916 (iwm: Q1523)

buried there demanded reverence for their efforts on our behalf (Picture 44). Even with other visitors there was virtually no discernable sound. I had noticed this deep silence once before when visiting Dachau.

The remnant of its devastating past is the surrounding countryside that is blighted by the many hillocks now so green but once dangerous shell craters and maybe still containing unexploded ordnance. There is absolutely no way one can really imagine this battlefield as it was on 1st July 1916 (Picture 45). Standing on the rocky Caribou vantage point, facing the uneven fields across which the Essex men along with others went into a hail of devastating machine gun fire, we tried to imagine what it was like. Try as we might we just cannot ever really wear our ancestors' shoes.

This peaceful setting with its thick fir trees denies the conditions on that initially sunny morning: the furious ear-splitting noise of exploding shells, the propelling shrapnel balls, cordite-filled air, the chaos and confusion, the crying and dying of the wounded, the blood, gore and guts of decaying bodies, the shouting, the smell of fear and dread of the costly carnage that so swiftly turned the field into a wilderness of blue grey starkness of petrified foliage. By all accounts it was literally hell on earth but even that description has lost its full emotive power by its overuse through the years since The Somme.

The Newfoundland Memorial is a forty acre site that has preserved the battleground with its various trenches and numerous shell craters now verdant mounds and is dedicated to the memory of the 1st Newfoundland Battalion who suffered high casualties within thirty minutes of their advance.

Gough (2004) argues that those who chose the site and organised its landscape contrived to produce an historical narrative that gives priority to some memories over others. This is partly understandable as the Newfoundland sacrifice particularly helped to forge that small Dominion's identity but others also suffered that morning. The 1st Essex has no specific memorial.

Thiepval Memorial

Nearby there is the impressively tall Thiepval Memorial on the D73, next to the village of Thiepval, off the main Bapaume to Albert Road (D929). Set high on a ridge overlooking the surrounding countryside it records the names of the 73,357 missing British and South African soldiers with no known grave and can be seen for quite a few miles around poignantly reminding us all of the ultimate sacrifice made by those courageous sons of the Empire. Each year a major ceremony is held at the memorial on 1st July.

46. Looking up to Thiepval Memorial Arch

Standing there and looking up under the imposing arch (Picture 46) it exuded a stark yet spiritual presence that rightly demanded our respect. Walking around in the slightly damp yet crisp air and scanning those thousands of names, each with a grieving family, I began to feel a melancholy resentment about the unnecessary loss of that generation of young men.

Monchy-le-Preux

Monchy is a typically small French village just off the D939-A1/E15 junction. Like so many of the battle sites, it had the unfortunate fate to be atop a high ridge that dominated the surrounding countryside for many miles. It is because of this strategic position close to Arras it became the location of a desperate chapter in that larger battle in April 1917. A macabre fact is that the remains of dead soldiers are still being found in the fields around the whole Arras area by local farmers these many years on.

We arrived there at about 3pm and found the place strangely deserted apart from the odd car or two passing through. On a rising hill, opposite the village school, there is another striking Caribou Memorial to the Newfoundlanders above what was a German ruin. Just a bit up that road

47. 37th Division Memorial at Monchy-le-Preux

there is the church which has the village memorial in the space in front. There is a memorial to the 37th Division a few hundred yards up that road but it is very close to the road (Picture 47). Parking is available just below the Caribou on the same side of the road diagonally opposite the school. The British Cemetery is to the south of the village, north of D939.

To the south east is the land where the Essex fought desperately to hold the village in the inevitable counterattack. Driving around the various roads leading into Monchy one easily appreciates why this part of the larger Arras battle was so vital.

Cambrai

As an engagement, Cambrai suffers somewhat from the Somme and Ypres 'effect'. However, it was just as important and is distinguished by being the first integrated attack including massed ranks of tanks. The bridge at Masnières, on the D644 crossing the St Quentin Canal, is just a couple of miles south west of Cambrai which is situated a few yards from the original 1917 bridge (Picture 48).

48. Masnières Bridge today

This bridge was the objective set for 1st Essex to capture but the first tank crossing it caused it to partially collapse and, as discussed elsewhere in the Cambrai section, the attack was held up. They later subdued a German battery at La Vacquerie, further south on the canal. Nowadays, it looks just like a normal road bridge over a canal giving no hint of its historic past.

Loker/Ypres

On route to Ypres, about 6 miles west, we called into the tiny village of Loker which, like so many places in Flanders, has its own war cemetery (Picture 49).

49. Loker Hospice Cemetery, Flanders

Buried there is great uncle Edgar, the only Bailey brother to lose his life in the Great War. The notorious Passchendaele was a series of linked engagements in the whole of the Ypres area and he was killed in one of these battles south of Ypres near to Hollebeke. Loker Hospice Cemetery is in the middle of a field just behind the main street and across from the Hospice which tended to the wounded from 1917 onwards.

Standing there in the late afternoon looking at Edgar's gravestone, I was struck with a mounting respect for both him and also the people responsible for the war cemeteries dotted all over Picardie and Flanders. Later, passing through the next village towards Ypres, we stopped off for a much-needed beer in a local bar. The English-speaking son told us the local people also contributed to the upkeep of the cemetery in gratitude to the allied troops who liberated Belgium. We were struck by this contemporary acknowledgement of events that preceded him by two generations.

Ypres was another strategically placed centre which stood in the path of the German advance in 1914. Now Ieper (in Flemish/Dutch), it was where the first poison gas attack on the Western Front occurred in 1915 but the Germans failed to take it. As a result of early allied capture it was continuously subjected to a series of furious assaults by heavy artillery, including *"Big*

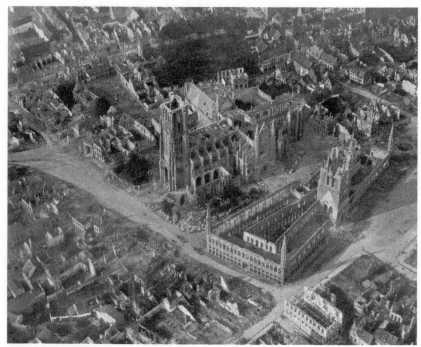

50. Ypres in rubble

Bertha", which completely destroyed it leaving it a pile of rubble as the picture clearly demonstrates (Picture 50).

After the war it was built again from scratch almost as a replica of the original city with money from German reparations and emerged as a

51. Warming up at the Menin Gate 1917

beautifully arranged town centre with a medieval and contemporary feel. It is now dubbed Peace City.

We arrived late afternoon and booked into a small hotel on D'Hondtstraat, merely 300 odd yards from the Market Square and the Menenpoort, or Menin Gate. During the war it was not actually a gate but a destroyed gap in the east of the city wall (Picture 51) through which thousands of allied troops passed on their way to the front, many to never return.

Every evening at 8 o'clock the traffic through the gate is temporarily stopped and various wreaths are laid and then the Last Post is sounded in tribute to the dead by buglers of the local Volunteer Fire Brigade. The locals respect this interruption and are proud of those Empire troops who fell defending their city, claiming them as their own. That evening it was packed with onlookers and one could hardly move. It was a profoundly poignant and reflective moment made all the more so by the participation of three Royal Newfoundlanders.

It is definitely something to be recommended to everyone because it keeps alive the memory of the 54,896 who died there between August 1914 and 15th August 1917. Those who died after that date are buried in Tyne Cot Cemetery just off the N332 at Zonnebeke, close to Passchendaele.

Langemarck

To the east of Ypres are a plethora of war cemeteries and memorials dedicated to British and Commonwealth soldiers and they really require a few days to visit and appreciate them properly. As this story has concentrated on Frank Bailey and the Essex, so it is that Langemarck features in their history. Just off N313 leaving Ypres, it was the scene of a ferocious battle which the British eventually won. Casualties on both sides were numerous and this is evinced by the large German Cemetery there. One interesting feature is the

sculpture of four striking life-size bronze statues of soldiers standing in mourning on the edge of the cemetery as if on the horizon (Picture 52). The 1st Essex played a vital part in the taking of Langemarck and that site

52. Life size bronze soldiers at Langemarck German Cemetery

has special significance as this is the area where Frank was gassed although knowing exactly where this happened has proved impossible. The legacy of the regiment is evident from the traditional naming of places occupied, as that of "Essex Farm" demonstrates.

Passchendaele/Tyne Cot

This location is notorious for reasons that need little elaboration. This was the site of a battle memorable for being even bloodier than The Somme and with added life-threatening mud. What must it have been like trying to manoeuvre heavy equipment around in the knee-deep particularly glutinous Passchendaele mud? This was chillingly brought home to me in the merest way whilst slipping around when dog walking in a muddy field.

Indeed, as an officer wrote (in Burrows) at the time:

> "In wet weather there was imminent danger of death from suffocation to any man who slipped off into the beastly slime. At times during a spell of fine weather the partially dried-up shell holes revealed the mutilated remains of what had once been men. It was Dante's Inferno and Bunyan's Valley of the Shadow of Death rolled into one."

Tyne Cot, just south of the village of Passendale off the N303, is the largest Commonwealth Cemetery and is not only impressive in its overwhelming size but distinctive in design with a quarter moon rotunda shape at one end. The Cross of Sacrifice (Picture 53) was originally built around a German pillbox that was used as an advance first aid station.

Tyne Cot Cemetery commemorates over 11,900 buried soldiers and a further 34,000 plus of those missing with no known grave, all of whom were engaged in the Ypres salient after 15th August 1917. Adding these numbers to those commemorated on the panels of the Menin Gate gives us the true extent of the colossal British Commonwealth losses sustained at Passchendaele.

On a final note, so many years have passed since these historic battles and they are so deeply embedded in our national consciousness that any personal comments on the sites of remembrance inevitably end up only regurgitating the available vocabulary. That cannot be helped but the result is that the words we resort to can no longer capture the ghastly scale, horror and obscenity of that war.

Having said that, my visits to these sites have reinvigorated my knowledge of our history and generated a greater sense of utter admiration and respect

53. Cross of Sacrifice, Tyne Cot Cemetery

for those young men who answered the call of their country and died in the process, not least one of my family. We owe it to every one of them to keep their memory alive forever and hope that our children and grandchildren never ever face the same fate.

Coda

THE 1ST Bn Essex Regiment was always in there at the kill taking part in all the major campaigns of the Great War, very often from the very first attacks. They were at Gallipoli, from the first to the end, at The Somme on that first dreadful sunny morning at Beaumont Hamel, at Arras playing a large part in saving Monchy-le-Preux, in the dangerous drowning mud at Passchendaele and at the famous tank battle at Cambrai.

However, in the course of this search into the career of Frank Bailey and his Battalion, I have found that they have been either superficially mentioned at these engagements or basically ignored. One case in point is when consulting specialist books on Gallipoli and The Somme there was not even a mention of 1st Essex in the index!

Taking Gallipoli first, when that place name crops up the first thought that immediately jumps into most minds is of the legendary ANZAC Cove and how the Australasian troops suffered from being landed by bad intelligence on the most inappropriate terrain. Their contribution is widely recognised and quite rightly so but, mainly as a result of the 1981 film 'Gallipoli', their deeds have overshadowed other equally brave contributions from British and other allied units at Cape Helles.

Australian author and filmmaker Harvey Broadbent (2005) endorses this view succinctly when he says: "*When I first came to the Australian Gallipoli story as an immigrant to this country in 1975 I was struck, not just by its place as an agent in forging national identity, but also by its exclusivity. Many Australians I spoke to were not or hardly aware that the British and French were present in far larger numbers, let alone Indian and French colonial troops. This impression was further strengthened by Peter Weir's Australian ethnocentrically influential film, Gallipoli, in 1981. The trend continued - so much so – that some British commentators have accused Australia of 'hijacking' the Gallipoli story.*"

Even within the British contribution the same oversight seems to occur. The 1st Lancashire Fusiliers are quite rightly lauded for their gallant action on the first morning of the attack and the VCs they earned *"before breakfast"*, facing the most withering firepower that killed 183 and wounded 279 of their 950-strong battalion. This earned them the honour of having the W Beach named *"Lancashire Landing"* after their exploits but ironically, unlike the ANZAC beach, this name was not to survive in official circles. Nevertheless, their memorial sited nearby retains this honoured title.

This rightfully gives the Lancashire men due recognition but where are the 1st Essex in all this? It is almost as if they were *not* there. Indeed, rigorous investigation into diverse records stubbornly failed to make the obvious connections between 1st Essex and W Beach that one would expect. Notable exceptions are useful overlaps between Major Gillam's dairy (1918), giving an excellent first-hand account during the campaign, and John Burrows' (1931) book which is specifically about the 1st Battalion in the Great War anyway. Even in Broadbent's excellent and well balanced attempt to redress the ANZAC bias there is scant mention.

As an historical fact, the equally courageous men of the 1st Bn Essex were also on W Beach to reinforce the Lancashire Fusiliers and giving of their best in the face of the same enemy firepower, losing just on 100 men. They also featured in other actions on the peninsula and in the numerous later Battles of Krithia and Suvla Bay.

This same problem also applies to the role played by the 1st Essex men during the initial part of The Somme Offensive. Somehow, once again in a reprise of Gallipoli, they are almost invisible from the records although they were clearly in action on the first day at Beaumont Hamel. Here, they have been overshadowed by another regiment albeit by the very deserving troops of the Newfoundland and their dreadful losses in a doomed advance.

Nevertheless, in that same attack, the Essex men also sustained considerable losses although fewer than their dominion comrades. They suffered from the same misunderstanding of orders and had to negotiate the same communications trench but fortunately their greater experience told in maintaining their cover for longer whilst moving up to the front line. When they did go in the open they suffered the same devastating machine gun and small arms fire. Remember the 949 Essex soldiers commemorated at the Thiepval Memorial.

All the brave men who gave their lives defending the allied cause rightfully deserve our gratitude and full recognition. Although it is understandable that some units will capture the public imagination for their heroic deeds more than others we should not let it obscure the contribution of those others, in this case 1st Bn Essex Regiment. The men from Newfoundland attract much attention because, like the ANZACs at Gallipoli, they were from the Empire and it was their first contribution to the war. In the case of Newfoundland, this sparsely populated island could only raise one battalion of volunteers for the war effort so the losses felt were proportionately greater. Another factor is undoubtedly the striking post-war Caribou Memorials particularly at Beaumont Hamel.

This book records and honours the service of Major Frank Bailey, his brothers and the 1st Essex who gave their all to their country in battlefields far from their home county. In his 1923 Preface, Burrows wrote of: "*... armies made up of tough, simple fighters like the men of Essex; always relied upon to do their best, to fill the breach; then often yielding to others in pride of place in despatches.*"

In the Forward to Burrows, Ian Hamilton, ironically C-in-C at Gallipoli concurs: "*If the County of Essex was moved away to the North or the West or put into Ireland or France, someone would stick up a statue or something to those fellows.*" What a very good idea even though it is 90 years late. Like the Newfoundlanders they certainly also deserve specific memorials at these places including Beaumont Hamel.

54. Algy Wood, left, with Huge Bowen and Capt. Dinan in 1914

Appendix A

Search Diary

2005
Oct ½-term
> Attempt to locate Frank's *London Gazette* DCM entry for younger son's school WW1 France/Flanders battlefields project without any luck. All other agencies
> – hard to make contact and elicit replies by email or phone!

2006
Nov   A quest initiated for details of his military service retriggered by Remembrance Week Gallipoli TV programme. Ann prods me to follow up on Frank's military career properly this time. Going for it

22nd   Email letter to Keeper, Essex Regiment Museum (ERM)
         Reply letter from ERM with database/explanation: most helpful! Ian Hook (IH) asks: 'Did grandfather have a brother Ernest, the Drum Major of the Regiment?'

29th   Rely thanking him, asking for more info and answering his Q in the negative

December
1st   Wrote to *London Gazette*, Gallipoli Association (GA) & Ministry of Defence (MOD) Personnel Centre

6th   *London Gazette* replied with front page and DCM award entry

16th   Wrote *Essex Chronicle* ref some newspaper articles

19th   Wrote Imperial War Museum (IWM)

28th   *Essex Chronicle* replied. No records there so contact Chelmsford Library: wrote to them

2007
January
2nd   GA PR Officer replies with info, refers me to War Diaries

5th   Chelmsford Library replied with brief cutting (thanks) suggesting I contact ERM!

8th   IWM replied giving some useful background references and inviting me to use Reading room

9th   Contacted GA, PR Officer about the 2nd Tuesday of month meeting, at The National Archive (TNA) at Kew. He'll wear a strikingly striped GA tie and be in café

11th   Wrote IH asking for more information and suggesting a meeting at ERM

19th   Emailed IH requesting photos. Replied, saying museum moving records so wait a few weeks

20th   Wrote to Royal Anglian Regiment (RAR) HQ, Warley; Emailed letter to Western Front Association (WFA)

21st   Essex WFA emailed reply with information offering me Vol. 7, 1st Battalion narrative: there's a grainy photo of RSM/WO1 Frank Bailey!

25th   RAR replied referring me to MOD Mailpoint 400 and referring me back to IH (he's obviously the man!)

February

13th   TNA, Kew to meet GA man but couldn't find him anyway, despite the tie! Scanned 'burnt records', no luck, only to be told later on enquiry that post-1923 personnel are with MOD in Edinburgh: waste of time!

March

19th   Follow-up letter chasing non-reply from MOD

April

-July   An intensive period of reading to provide background

August

16th   Finally met IH at ERM: proves an exponentially helpful session and also interesting chat about '60's music

17th   Wrote to *Illustrated London News* (ILN) asking for a double-spread picture of the Gallipoli landings

29th   Phoned *Guardian* newspaper to contact freelance critic Mick M (long lost first cousin with Frank's full and dress medals), spoke to someone who gave me Human Resources & Guide extensions; phoned those and left message

September

1st   Emailed *Guardian* with attached enquiry letter for Mick M

3rd   Another follow-up letter to MOD! Wrote *Guardian* newspaper, still seeking to contact Mick M

7th Letter from MOD saying they hadn't received any previous correspondence of 1/12/06, 19/3/07! Gives info on how to apply for service records

October

1st Replied to MOD applying and paying £30 for Frank Bailey's records

11th Paid ILN for Gallipoli picture

19th Letter from MOD acknowledging receipt of application and cheque and saying search can take from 4-5 months!

December

12th Letter and military records received from MOD and info about MOD Medal Office. Important discoveries! MOD papers reveal Frank's elder brother Ernest also in 1st Essex, immediately phone IH and he emails Ernest's ERM data by return. A whole new avenue opens up: where will it lead?

2008

January

5th Tried to contact Joan S (website inoperative) so wrote seeking any possible info about Frank & Ernest

8th Wrote MOD asking if they could locate Ernest's records on the back of Frank's; wrote to IWM requesting appointment to use Reading Room, received letter from MOD Medal Office giving info on how to access medals: basically you have to purchase duplicates from "*reputable medal dealers*"

11th Reply from MOD with Ref. No. for Ernest for completely new search: another £30! (They're *my* relatives!)

11th Ordered Burrow's 1st Essex book, a vital source with much detail to complement my findings

14th IWM reply arranging use of Reading Room: Gillam diary & Martin useful data

16th 2nd visit to TNA to rescan burnt records either side of previous microfilm for Baileys: still no luck!

18th Wrote to Chris Baker (his 1418 site not working!) inquiring about role of NCOs in action

21st Ordered 2 more relevant books online

23rd Emailed seeking Mick M's address with letter at Guardian

25th Visited IWM, consulted in Reading Room

31st Emailed *Essex Chronicle* for (free) advert seeking any info on Frank and Ernest

March

5th   TNA and discovered 1881 Census entries for 7 Bailey Bros! (2 were in army) ... the trail expands into the unknown

6th   Emailed IH about other brothers possible service, replied with some Edgar info ... very useful, he died in 1917, probably 3rd Ypres and buried at Loker Hospice nearby, my Frank 'n' Ernest advert appears in *Essex Chronicle*, p.24

10th   Ordered Ernest's birth certificate from General Register Office (GRO) website

12th   GRO sends Ernest's birth certificate
Ordered Edgar's death cert from GRO

19th   Wrote MOD instituting search for Ernest docs; wrote Chelmsford Library for *Essex Chronicle* entry about Edgar's death

21st   Wrote to *Times* for similar entry Edgar's entry

26th   Wrote to a Joan S (KIA site), again seeking any info about Edgar's death (no reply)

29th   Received MOD (26th March) reply about Ernest's records ... owing to high volume of urgent requests likely to be 4-5 months ... they said that last time but it didn't take that long

31st   Chelmsford Library reply with Edgar's death notice in *Essex Chronicle*

April

3rd   Emailed Essex Records Office (ERO) about Bailey brothers

21st   Resigned p/t college job to concentrate on grandad project

25th   Received ERO letter with copy of their email reply to mine (4th April 11.07) which I didn't receive! Info given about accessing parish records and Essex Census returns – may do

28th   Travelled to family grave, Woodman Road, Brentwood (photo) then onto West Bergholt, Colchester, to see Edgar's Memorial at parish church. No luck – it's inside locked church. Called in at ERM to donate Frank's retirement silver salver and useful chat with IH who knew of many of the signatories

29th   Emailed West Bergholt Parish Council to ask about the Edgar Memorial, accessed free 14-day trial on Ancestry, completed boxes for Bailey siblings on family tree owned by a Jane CK (not a Bailey? Probably married name)

30th   New International Newspapers Ltd replied unable to locate Edgar's death notice – typical!

May

1st   Jane C (née Bailey and great granddaughter of Ernest!) rang and we shared an exponential information chat, re-accessed Bailey tree and downloaded most photos of my newly discovered extended family; Hugh of West Bergholt PC called just after and offered to take photo of Edgar's Memorial in St Mary's Church, West Bergholt. What a couple of breakthroughs and all within the hour!

Emailed IH with this updated information, he later rang and chatted about significance of Charles Bailey in uniform photo and how these old photos could be enhanced and possibly enlarged

2nd   Emailed Jane to double check some of the facts discussed on phone yesterday

Wrote to *Essex Family History* journal inquiring about adverts

3rd   Jane emails vital information and in response to specific questions will send some detailed stuff through pretty soon

5th-23rd A useful ongoing mutual exchange of family data with Jane by email/phone

28th   Travelled to Colchester first thing to visit Fordham ... couldn't get bus – only one a day! 10.00 taxi to Fordham, 3-4 miles outside city and many Bailey graves there in All Saints Churchyard, behind Three Horseshoes pub. Placed advert card in village PO, took photos of village green and sign – pleasantly rural – so small it hardly qualifies as a village really, walked through to All Saints Churchyard, checked and took photos of gravestones. Went for a pint at 11.15am while waiting for return taxi but pub closed weekdays! Fully understand why Bailey brothers hoofed it off to army, America and anywhere!

Went on to meet old friend at Colchester Real Ale Festival

29th   *Essex Family History* reply explaining advert details

31st   Phone message from Marlene (Local History Society) had seen my card in Fordham PO, told me she was at school with 'Granville' (Jane's dad) and great uncle Ernie was local postman in '50s. She remembered him as Chelsea Pensioner and will send some info by post (he wasn't & she never did!)

June

2nd   Email from Jane explaining about her grandma Irene (Ernest's 2nd daughter)

An email from Lorna F to Jane she received about the upcoming

Firmin reunion

Joe Firmin rang, had seen my letter in West Bergholt Parish Magazine, Firmin-Bailey plethora of info. poured out:

Sarah Harriet, Frank's older sister was his granny! She married John Thomas Firmin 1884, had many kids, died 1952 (census said 1950?), also remembered older brother Charles Porter as businessman and 1st wife was known as Patsy, Elizabeth was his (great) Auntie Lizzie who went to USA and married an oyster merchant in New York, when he died she came home and died in Fordham 1955, told me 1944 army story about my RSM grandad telling him off on parade ground (he was a Major then and not in Essex but never mind, am keeping open mind), he'll send me an RSM Frank photo

3rd   Posted advert seeking Bailey info with *Essex County Standard* website, acknowledged in 10min, wrote to Joe Firmin with Bailey search summary and some photos

4th   Rec'd letter from Joe Firmin explaining relations and promising photos

9th   Joe's follow-up letter with loads of Firmin family info and a superb clear photo of RSM Bailey: brilliant!

17th   Joe Firmin letter with material about his uncles' WW1 military service and his father's WW1 wounding: very interesting

18th   Rec'd Ernest's MOD records. Another Joe letter outlining his WW2 records: first hand & fascinating, wrote back to attaching ERM data on military service of his uncles and father

21st   Joe wrote thanking me for data and promising to dig out anything relevant

28th   Planned reunion weekend cancelled because of Ben Firmin's serious illness (couldn't have gone anyway)

July

1st   Doris (Ernest's eldest) phoned ... a long informative chat about Frank & Ernest

2nd   Wrote to Doris with some photos and further info

3rd   Doris parcel arrived, very interesting Ernest army info and some extended family Birth, Marriage & Death certs

4th   Phoned Doris thanking her for package and another long chat ... will visit her to return material but have to wait until school holidays as she's child minding her granddaughter's kids

Phoned Joe Firmin for some more detailed info about his extended family ... obliged with full list of Sarah Harriet's children, with Dates of Birth & Dates of Death (taken from the front of the bible she gave him as a kid).

Reminder: she was his granny and eldest sister of Frank, my grandad

7th   Phoned IH ... not in an office so gave me mobile no. ... phoned it later but cut off mid-speech ... tried again and cut off yet again – mid-flow ... texted him a couple of times but no response (Days later he told me that it had died and T-mobile hadn't delivered the promised replacement ... 21st C technology, eh?)

8th   Emailed IH at ERM about phone link and with some Qs about MOD records as I finish off Frank's army story

12th   No reply from IH, so assume the 'move' taking up time ... can't get through on phone

15th   Emailed IH to ask if online yet

17th   Still no response so rang ERM office ... a couple of times ... no reply ... third time ... secretary said he was off work today but hasn't had any office or internet connection for last couple of weeks: that explains it

18th   Rang ERM again and left message ... IH at lunch but will ring back ... rang back ... long chat about some questions I asked ... his info. is always very detailed and helpful

Rang Doris about visiting her next week but she said kids didn't break up 'til following week: can't wait

22nd   Phoned IH at ERM ... at a meeting but told to phone his new office number after 2pm ... had chat ... they're still in the middle of a big move and reorganisation ... tried again

24th   Phoned IH ... out to lunch ... calls back ... has found a Cpl Cooper's diary of 1st Bn in Ireland ... mentions RSM Frank and Sgt Drummer Ernest several times ... emails it ... it's in a long column format ... takes up about 750 pages and all over the shop, so I reformatted it and tried to make it more readable by a bit of reorganisation, e.g. spacing etc

25th   Emailed & phoned IH ... some urgent questions and about Cpl Cooper's diary ... yet another useful chat and answers to some key army procedural questions

27th   Called Doris to confirm visit tomorrow

28th   Visited Doris in Borehamwood and had a long family history discussion leaving with high quality photos

29th   Emailed Jane with some photos taken yesterday

August

17th   Visits to Copford, Fordham & West Bergholt, cleaned & took photos of Charles & Martha, Oliver and Eva gravestones ... can't find Ernest's headstone anywhere despite thorough search

19th   Emailed photos of Doris' old house 'Fossetts' ... hardly changed

28th   Off through Eurotunnel to France for Beaumont Hamel, Thiepval (so many lost!), Monchy-le-Preux, Cambrai and onto Belgium to find Edgar's grave in Loker ... found it in a small well-kept graveyard in the middle of a field

Flowers, photos, then onto Ypres via much needed beers. Attend the 8pm Menin Gate Last post ceremony ... moving and thought provoking, dinner under floodlit Cloth Hall in town square

29th   Off to Langemarck ... endless driving around ... these Belgian signs are weird ... even asking directions didn't work so no luck on Langemarck ... onto Zonnebeck/Passchendaele ... while there pick up Archive material ... must return soon ... listen to ODI cricket on 198 to Bruges square for lunch ... then back to Calais

31st   Email photos to Doris, Jane and Ian ... some techno-problems!

September

1st   Doris didn't get them ... on checking email address realise it is one letter out!

2nd   IH mail to advise him about chasing up Ernest grave details: he advises about possible CWGC 'deal'

3rd   All cleared up and photos delivered to Doris, talked on phone and find that Ernest grave has no headstone! No wonder I couldn't find it

4th   Jane called and discussed gravestone for Ernest ... yes we'll sort it when it's found

5th   Emailed Passchendaele Archives with Edgar info to establish when and how of death

9th   Phone IH for pre-TNA visit advice and get useful tips

10th   Visit to TNA ... very frustrating, against all odds cannot find any trace of Charles' or Edgar's army records

11th   Emailed IH who said the files wouldn't tell me much more than I already know, emailed again to check some facts

12th   IH reply with information

15th   Started writing up all recently gained information

17th   Emailed IH yet again to double check some facts for book and inquire about some possible recorded discrepancies

22nd   IH reply clarifying discrepancies

29th   Emailed IH seeking more clarifications about MOD entries

October

1st   Holiday

13th   IH helpful replies to my questions

14th   Start final write up

23rd   Emailed IH brief question

24th   Emailed IH another discrepancy

27th   Emailed IH and reply to question about an old photo: is it Charles or Frank? Points to Frank by age and MI uniform

28th   Phoned Brentwood photograph shops hopefully chasing up photo: no luck and one shut

30th   Phoned final photo shop as last resort: again no luck but gave me idea about possible source ... must follow up

31st   Finished writing ... collated, printed and photocopied

November

2nd   Surprise and welcome email from Passchendaele Archives with some details of where and how Edgar died ... included it in relevant part ... JIT!

Appendix B

BAILEY BROTHERS DIARY

Frank, *Ernest & Edgar (Italics)*

1897

22/2	*Ernest enlisted 18 years 3 months (4810) Colchester, serving in the Militia, posted Essex Regiment (He was actually 19 years 5 months)*

1901

25/1	Queen Victoria died
12/3	Frank enlisted 18 years 3 months (6380), London, posted Warley (Essex Regiment HQ) for 8 months training
7/7	Posted to 1st Battalion, Essex
26/11	Posted to South Africa, served with a Mounted Infantry Company
2/12	Mounted Infantry Certificate, Aldershot
6/12	*Ernest Bailey to South Africa*
15/12	Appointed L-Cpl

1902

26/6	Represented Essex Regiment at Edward VII Coronation
22/7	*Ernest transferred 1st Bn*
24/7	Posted as Private to 2nd Bn
14/8	*Ernest back from South Africa*
15/8	*Ernest posted to India*
Sept.	L-Cpl in 2nd Bn
16/10	Left South Africa
17/10	Home, appointed Acting Cpl (on L-Cpl's pay)

1903

6/3	Posted as Private, 1st Bn to India
25/5	Granted PG Pay (A motivational penny a day gratuity if no crimes committed)
22/12	Awarded 2nd Class Certificate of Education

1904

8/3	Passed exams for rank of Cpl
7/4	Extended service to complete 8 years service with the Colours
4/7	*Ernest permitted to extend his service to complete 12 years with the colours*
10/5	*Ernest appointed Driver*

1906

5/1	Promoted to Corporal
16/7	Transport Duties, Certificate awarded, Bangalore
30/10	Promoted to Lance Sergeant, continuing service in India
14/12	Posted Burma

1907

Mar:	Invalided home (no reason stated) joined 2nd Bn, served in Dublin and Curragh Camp, Ireland
24/7	Extended service to 12 years

1908

3/3	British India Service (Indian Army)
11/3	Home and posted to Ireland
25/3	Posted to 2nd Bn, volunteered for Foreign Service again
16/9	*Ernest to India Service*
27/10	*Ernest appointed L-Cpl*

1909

18/2	*Ernest in Essex ERG as L-Cpl, B Company, 1st Bn, received 3rd Class Education Cert*
12/11	Joined 1st Bn at Quetta, India, as L-Sgt

1910

9/10	L-Sgt Frank married Rosanne Howe in Karachi

1911

1/1	*Ernest "brought in on the paid establishment" as L-Cpl*
	Ernest photographed in Quetta as Acting Corporal in Regimental Hockey team
20/4	Promoted to Sgt
10/5	Re-engaged as Sgt, A Company (Coy), 1st Bn for 21 years service
15/6	Son: Frederick, William Charles, born, Quetta (my father)

30/8   Appointed Orderly Room Cpl

1912

26/3   Awarded Army School 1st Class (Group I), Quetta

24/9   Awarded 1st Class Certificate of Education

1913

19/4   Appointed Orderly Room Sgt, in Mauritius at Bn HQ

25/11   Colonial relief expedition in Mauritius until 6/12; *Ernest Bailey promoted to Cpl (ERG)*

7/12   Posted Mauritius for 1 year, *Ernest also*

1914

20/1   *Ernest Bailey promoted unpaid L-Sgt (ERG)*

8/12   1st Bn home to Warley Barracks (both brothers)

1915

21/3   Set sail for Dardanelles

23/3   Posted MEF, embarked at Avonmouth

8/4   *Ernest appointed paid L-Sgt*

24/4   Sailed for Gallipoli

25/4   Gallipoli: landed 'W' beach at Cape Helles in X Coy at around 10.00 hours to reinforce Lancashire Regiment who had taken massive casualties; *Ernest also landed W beach with W Coy*

2/5   Lt Col Owen Godfrey Faussett, Commanding Officer, 1st Bn, killed in action, Gallipoli

9/5   *Ernest Bailey, with W Coy, received gunshot wound in arm (1st Bn War Diary, MOD record)*

15/5   Appointed Acting RSM in field

4/6   *Ernest promoted Sgt*

13/7   *Ernest posted home*

27/7   *Ernest posted depot, 3rd Bn*

15/5   Confirmed Acting RSM in Alexandria

15/8   Promoted RSM/Warrant Officer Class I (WO1) in Alexandria

4/9   Proceeded to join Bn

27/9   Joined Bn at Gallipoli

30/10   Caught Major Wood, Adjutant, as he fell back shot dead by a sniper (Burrows: 199)

1916

8/1	Took part in evacuation from Gallipoli Peninsula
15/3	Embarked Alexandria for France
20/3	Landed at Marseilles
21/3	Posted BEF, France
2/4	Leave to UK
23/4	Attended a Course of Introduction at Flexicourt, France
23/5	Rejoined Bn in the field
24/5	*Ernest embarked*
25/5	*Ernest landed in France*
1/6	*Ernest appointed Sgt-Drummer to 1st Bn*
6/6	*Ernest joined 1st Bn in field*
1/7	Battle of the Somme (Beaumont Hamel), as RSM organising men to achieve objectives
23/10	Leave to UK
23/11	Leave to UK

1917

22/3	Embarked for England for posting to Home establishment
9/4	Mentioned in Field Marshal Haig's dispatches "*for distinguished and gallant services and devotion to duty*: Bailey, 6380, RSM, F."
14/4	Aided defence of left flank of Monchy-le-Preux with Lt Lawson, Adjutant (Burrows: 221)
25/5	Haig Dispatch in *London Gazette*: "*for distinguished and gallant services and devotion to duty.*"
27/6	Leave to UK
7/7	Back with 1st Bn
23/7	Awarded Serbian Cross of Kara-George, 1st Class, with Swords, recorded in *London Gazette*
7/8	Field Ambulance, admitted with 'myalgia', to 14th Corps Rest Stn
13/8	*Driver Edgar Bailey (163562),Royal Field Artillery, dies of wounds, buried Row 1B: 25, at Loker Hospice Cemetery, near Ypres, Flanders and also commemorated on Church Memorial in St Mary the Virgin, West Bergholt, near Colchester, Essex*
28/8	Rejoined Bn
15/9	*Edgar's death recorded in 'The Times', London*
21/9	*Edgar's death recorded in 'Essex Chronicle', leaves Eva widow and 3 children*
26/9	Wounded by gas attack at Langemarck, Flanders, remained at duty

20/11	Battle of Cambrai, France, starts with first massed use of tanks
	Awarded DCM, full citation in *London Gazette*
13/12	To base for posting to Home establishment
15/12	Joined at Calais
22/12	Left France for England to Home Base
24/12	Home: posted "exchange" to another company
26/12	Depot at Warley

1918

5/1	Posted RSM, 2nd Bn (Training function)
12/1	Posted RSM, 4th Bn
2/2	Posted RSM, 3rd Bn
22/2	Posted RSM, 17th Bn
4/3	*London Gazette* DCM entry
30/9	Daughter (Rose Enid Muriel, aka 'Billy') born, Dedham, Nr. Colchester, Essex (my aunt)

1919

15/3	Posted RSM to Essex Depot, Warley
16/3	Posted RSM, 2nd Bn at Warley Depot
25/4	Posted RSM, 2nd Bn at Colchester
2/5	*Ernest posted from France*
8/5	*Ernest at Dispersal Centre, Purfleet*
16/5	Posted, 1st Bn
20/5	*Ernest transferred England, continuing beyond 21 years*
10/6	*Ernest posted to Depot*
14/7	Participated in Paris Victory Parade
27/8	Posted, 1st Bn
1/9	Posted to Ireland
10/10	*Ernest discharged Military Hospital, Colchester*
12/12	*Ernest Bailey Meritorious Service Medal award mentioned in 'London Gazette'*

1920

Serving with Major Arthur Percival, 1st Bn Intelligence Officer and Lt Frederick Clarke at Kinsale Barracks, Ireland

1921

19/3	The IRA engagement at Crossbarry
11/4	Permitted *"to continue in the service beyond 21 years"* as RSM
8/9	Took Adjutant's Parade
27/10	Another Adjutant's Parade 07.00-08.00
3/11	Took Sgt Majors' Parade
7/11	Supervised mass parade practising for Armistice march past, *Ernest in drum display*
6/12	Took combined parade at 11.30 until dinner time, Major Percival wearing swords, *Band also playing with Sgt-Drummer Ernest*
12/12	Another parade with NCOs 'passing out'
25/12	Christmas Dinner with issue of beer, RSM Bailey called for 'three cheers' for COs NCOs' and other ranks have seasonal drinks in RSM quarters

1922

4/1	Adjutant's parade taken by RSM
7/1	All married personnel left quarters except RSM
8/1	Left quarters
13/1	Drum parade beating the retreat 16.30-17.00 *with Ernest leading*
11-12/7	Officiating as 'Field Steward' for Sports
16/9	Posted to Bordon Camp, Hants

1923

11/1	Permitted *"to continue in the service beyond 21 years for an undefined period"* as RSM
31/8	*Ernest Bailey discharged as Sgt-Drummer with conduct 'exemplary' at Warley*
1/9	*Ernest Bailey received pension of 47½d per day*
30/11	Home
1/12	Granted a commission and promoted to Quartermaster (QM) and commissioned with rank of Lt at Warley Barracks

1925

20/3	Posted to Colchester

1929

4/4	1st Bn posted to Pembroke Dock

1931

13/3   At Warley

1/12   Promoted to Capt

1934

1/7   Promoted to Brevet Major

1935

Jan   In Saar, as part of League of Nations Force for monitoring of Plebiscite, 1st Bn patrols encounter Nazis parading around and some senior officers feel serious apprehension and alarm about another imminent war

1936

1/4   Promoted to Major

1937

12/12   Retired from Essex Regiment as Major (QM)

1939

14/2   Reemployed as Ordnance Officer Anti Aircraft (AA) Div, RAOC, at Warley

1941

1/4   Posted to AA, Ordnance Div, Mill Hill & area to fill vacancy for Ordnance Officer

1/5   Completed and signed Army Form B199a. Charles Bailey (elder brother) declared as 'Next-of-Kin or Guardian', living at: 'Belvedere, Halstead Road, Stanway, Colchester, Essex'

1942

28/3   Posted to No.1 Infantry Training Centre, Essex Regiment, WEF this date, having been granted 42 days notice leave

8/5   Struck off Strength No.1, ITC, on completion of 42 days notice leave, Home

1956

23/1   Frank died, Harold Wood Hospital, Essex, buried in Woodman Road Cemetery, Brentwood, Essex

1970

Ernest dies, buried in All Saints' Church Cemetery, Fordham, Essex

Appendix C

The Bandon Incident

John L. O'Sullivan, *Curious Journey: An Oral History of Ireland's Unfinished Revolution*, by Kenneth Griffith and Timothy O'Grady, (Mercier Press, 1998).

This is something that I haven't spoken about much. A war in any shape or form, it grows on you. When you are involved in active operations, it means you have to be disciplined and you have to face every circumstance as it comes. The decisions aren't always your own. This occasion I'm telling you about, I have never given it for publication to anybody, but I suppose our years are getting few and, as you say, it will give people an idea of the kinds of things we had to face and what we had to do about them.

During the height of the war, two members of the Essex Regiment were seen wandering around Bandon. At that time every stranger was under observation and people reported them to our command and they were captured. They claimed to be deserters, and while they said they were prepared to join our column and fight with us, they said they'd rather be sent back to England. Now we couldn't be sure what they were and they were taken to column headquarters to be interrogated. During the interrogation one of them said to the column commander – that was Tom Barry – he said he had a brother in the barracks in Bandon and that this brother wanted to get out too. This fellow thought the brother would be willing to work with us, and the idea of getting arms from Bandon barracks was discussed.

So arrangements were made and it was fixed up that members of the column would meet the brother at a particular place outside Bandon. Tom Barry was one of the men who was to go that night, but he was taken suddenly ill – he had a heart attack – and Captain John Galvin, Jim O'Donoghue, who was brigade assistant adjutant and Joe Begley were appointed to meet this fellow – I think he was a sergeant in the Essex Regiment. Well they went to the rendezvous and they were immediately pounced on by a section of the Essex Regiment. And they were given a terrible time, every bone in their body was broken before they were shot through the head. Somehow or other they were set up.

Now all during this time, the two others, the fellows who said they were deserters, were being held here in this house, my house here. They stayed here during the day and we had to shift them to another place at night. One of them was only nineteen or twenty and the other was older, maybe thirty or forty. My mother, God be good to her, she was a very motherly kind of person, and to her they were just people who were away from home, and she did her best for them. They had the same treatment, the same food as ourselves, maybe better. And we got on well with them too. We used to play cards with them at night.

Then after this murder of our people the order came through that the two prisoners were to be executed. They knew too much, they had talked with Barry and other people at our headquarters, and it was thought they might be intelligence officers as often happens in war when deserters go over to the enemy. We couldn't hold them as prisoners because that would be too dangerous, and the whole thing was looked at from every angle and it was decided to execute them. I wasn't there for this decision myself, but I can see now, looking back, that it was the only decision that could be made.

So anyway, we were told we were to dig a grave in a particular place. My brother came back home here for a pick and shovel and whatever was necessary. My mother was waiting – as she did whenever we were out, as all mothers do in troublesome times, when things were happening, when people who went out at nightfall never came back again, either killed in an ambush or taken prisoner or something – and she saw the pick and shovel going out and she probably sized up the situation and she said to my brother, 'Listen, Pat, don't ever do anything you'll be sorry for.' Well at that age – at any age – your mother is very important to you, and I can remember the weight of this thing on our minds as we were walking down the road with these two prisoners.

We told them we were sending them off by boat and all the time we were wondering what would we do about it. Finally I said to my brother, 'We'll have to get it postponed.'

So we took them up to the spot where the execution was supposed to be, and Moss Twomey was there – he was one of the officers in charge and he was a great friend of mine – and I said, 'They can't be shot tonight.' He said, 'It's very tough, but we have our orders and it must be done.' 'Well,' says I, 'it can't be done, for I'm bringing these fellows home or I'll be dead myself. I'll shoot the man who tries to stop us.' And I'd have done it too. But Twomey marched us up to the grave and just as we got there he said, 'About turn, quick march, take them back home. You'll get instructions where to take them tomorrow.'

So we brought them back home again, and the next night we were ordered to bring them out again. We were told then that they had to be shot, and the punishment we got for disobeying orders the previous night was that my brother and myself were appointed to the firing squad. My brother argued with them and said only one of us would do it, and it was settled that it would be him, because he was older. I think that a man that is in a firing squad should be a veteran who's had some experience of war. The revulsion of taking a human life goes very deep in a person, if he's been reared in a family.

So anyway the commanding officer —he was a different man from the night before – he said to the two prisoners, 'Now men,' he said, 'unfortunately we have to execute you. It won't be possible under the circumstances to get you a minister of religion, but we'll give you time to say your prayers and make your peace with God.' One of them said, 'We have no prayers to say.' 'Haven't you a soul?' said the commanding officer. 'I have,' he said and he lifted up his boot and he tapped at the bottom of it like that. 'That's all the sole I have,' he said. I'll never forget the blooming thing in my life. He faced it without a whimper. A man that could say that, you know now, before his death, and facing the bullet he must be a tough man. He was no ordinary solder. Now the likes of us, fighting for our country, we might face something like that. But an ordinary rank and file soldier in the British army hadn't that kind of commitment. They were shot there, anyway, the two of them together and buried on the spot.[1]

NOTE

1. This episode was later transformed by Frank O'Connor into a short story which following an account of the execution concludes: "I stood at the door, watching the stars and listening to the shrieking of the birds dying out over the bogs. It is so strange what you feel at times like that that you can't describe it. Noble says he saw everything ten times the size, as though there were nothing in the whole world but that little patch of bog with the two Englishmen stiffening into it, but with me it was as if the patch of bog where the Englishmen were was a million miles away and even Noble and the old woman, mumbling behind me, and the birds and the bloody stars were all far away, and I was somehow very small and very lost and lonely like a child astray in the snow. And everything that happened to me afterwards, I never felt the same about again."

   Tom Barry, who wrote briefly about the incident in his book Guerrilla Days in Ireland, betrayed no sentiments whatsoever about it: 'One of the oldest ruses in war is to send spies, posing as deserters into enemy lines. The classic example is, I think, the American Civil War, when hundreds of these pseudo-deserters were discovered as spies by both armies and dealt with as such. The two British spies (from the Essex Regiment) were brought to Kilbree, Clonakilty, and there they were executed."

Appendix D

1st BATTALION, ESSEX, BRIEF REGIMENT HISTORY

The 1st Battalion of The Essex Regiment was one with a long and distinguished record of military service. Below is a brief outline of their history.

The battalion was raised as an auxiliary "Regiment of Foot" by Royal Warrant in January 1741, during the War of the Austrian Succession, by a Col James Long of the 1st Foot Guards or Grenadier Guards. In those days regiments were named after their commander so naturally they were first known as "Long's Regiment". It comprised ten companies with 70 men in each with two drummers. They are believed to have originated in the southern counties.

Several ongoing changes affected the way these Foot Regiments were ranked and then named. One was that they were given numbers that represented their ranking in order of precedence, so Long's regiment was initially designated "The 55th Regiment of the Line" and under that name took an active part in the Jacobite Rebellion of 1745. It moved up the regimental rankings list, becoming the "44th" in 1748, as a result of other regiments being disbanded. Three years later regiments stopped being styled after their Colonel's names so it was now titled "The 44th Regiment of Foot".

Later on these units became linked to counties or localities. As the original colonel of the regiment had been born in East Ham the name was now the "44th" or "East Essex Regiment of Foot", colloquially known as "The Fighting Fours" or "Forty Fours".

The cap badge had the Sphinx above the word Egypt, representing the regiment's notable service there in the early Napoleonic occupation. The Castle and Key represent their association with Gibraltar Castle (Picture 55).

They served in many campaigns conducted as far and wide as North America, Flanders and the West Indies, including the famous capture of a French Eagle standard at the Battle of Salamanca in 1812, which adorns the colours and was subsequently incorporated into regimental symbolism.

The regiment was also involved in Napoleon's Hundred Days defeat at Quatre Bras, Waterloo, 1815. After that, peace dominated for nearly forty years until the Crimean War in 1854. However the regulars served in the colonies in Ireland, India, Assam, Burma, Gibraltar, Malta and Afghanistan.

55. *Essex Regiment Cap Badge*

Afghanistan

In 1841 the 44th, forerunners of 1st Battalion, were sent to Kabul the capital of Afghanistan then occupied by the British. In the 1st Afghan War there was a disaster when the Kabul Garrison under severe threat retired but was incessantly attacked and without supplies and wading in deep snow through the narrow passes for four days, was finally annihilated.

Crimea

The Crimean War against Russia started in 1854. The "44th" was one of the earliest units in the field something that has been an habitual part of its fighting history throughout its existence. It was awarded the battle honours for Alma, Inkerman and Sevastopol and Queen Victoria was so impressed with the troops in this war, she instituted the Victoria Cross in January 1856, which was allegedly forged from a captured Russian gun barrel. After Crimea, the "44th" was despatched as a reinforcement for the Indian Mutiny of 1857 but they arrived too late to be useful. In 1861, they saw action in North China.

Reorganisation

Eventually, under the Childers and Cardwell Reforms, each regiment was reconstituted as two line battalions, rotating one at home and the other abroad, with two militia battalions in reserve.

On 1st July 1881, they were informed that: "In future in all official documents the term "First Essex (late 44th) Regiment" will be used." Therefore the new Essex Regiment came into being and was formed by combining the 44th East Essex as the 1st Battalion with the 56th West Essex as 2nd Battalion. Warley Barracks, outside Brentwood in Essex, became the headquarters and depot for this regiment.

A long military presence had existed in Warley from 1742 whereby the common was used as a military camp, particularly in the summer months. This developed through the 1770s and became a permanent camp in 1804, at the start of the Napoleonic War. After their Chatham barracks became inadequate the Warley site was augmented by the transfer of the East India Company in 1843 and it was finally absorbed into the British Army in 1857.

In 1884, the 1st Battalion was part of a force which struggled up the Nile to relieve Khartoum and save General Gordon from the Mahdi who had overrun the Sudan.

Boer War

The Battalion gained battle honours for the Relief of Kimberley and the Battle of Paardeberg, in February 1900, and the famed bayonet charge at Driefontein. Of this charge, Leo Amery *The Times* Correspondent, said:

> "*There was a lull in the fighting as both sides braced themselves for the effort. Suddenly the Essex on the left sprang to their feet and raced forward. In a moment the whole line took the lead and went straight for the positions in front of them. In grim desperation, the Boers discharged their magazines, but there was no stopping the victorious infantry as it surged and over the low breastworks that had held it back for so many hours.*"[1]

Lieutenant Parsons, who had gained the fourth VC awarded to the

Regiment at Paardeberg, was cut down whilst leading his men with a demonstrable bravery that had earned him that medal in the first place.

From April 1901, the battalion was in charge of maintaining and defending the 'Blockhouse Line' along the road from Standerton to Ermelo, over 30 miles long.

These blockhouses, at intervals of about half a mile, were sturdily built in a combination of stone and iron protected by a low wall made from stone or sandbags and could house up to ten men partly dug in below the surface. They were to prevent the Boer farmers from crossing the line by stealth at night. A large force of Boers tried to do so a year later by attacking several blockhouse at once so as to cut through the wire but were repulsed by rapid fire. The battalion took the surrender of the enemy on the Ermelo line and thereafter helped to dismantle the blockhouse line.

1902-13

Between the end of the Boer War and outbreak of the Great War, the battalion was posted variously to India from September that year, Thayetmyo and Mandalay in Burma (1906-1908), back to India in 1908, half the battalion to Mauritius and half to South Africa in 1913, which is where they all were at the outbreak of war in August 1914.

1914-18

On 6th November 1914, HQ staff and the 'Mauritius' half of the battalion of 15 officers and 471 other ranks embarked on their journey to Plymouth to be reunited at Warley Barracks with the Durban half. The whole battalion, now with 28 Officers and 901 Other Ranks then went off to Harwich to join the 29th Division which comprised the 86th, 87th and 88th Brigades, made up from regulars brought home, mainly from India, with 1st Essex in the 88th.

The battalion arrived at Warwick on 5th March in preparation for active service. It was widely thought that the whole division was destined for France with the BEF where an offensive was being planned but instead it was sent with the MEF to the Middle East.

On 21st March, as part of 88th Brigade, the 1,000-strong battalion embarked at Bristol for Egypt. Only eleven days before they were due to land on the Gallipoli beaches they left for Mudros Harbour, on the island of Lemnos.

As part of the "*Incomparable 29th*" Division during the Great War (discussed in detail elsewhere) the 1st Essex served with the MEF at Cape

Helles, Krithia and Suvla Bay. With the BEF its record on the Western Front was equally significant. It was involved on 1st July 1916 in the Somme front at Beaumont Hamel. Owing to communication problems, the battalion took serious casualties when becoming stranded in No Man's Land supporting the 1st Newfoundland. It continued at the Somme until September.

In 1917, the battalion was extremely busy starting with Arras. It particularly distinguished itself at Monchy-le-Preux, Langemarck and Cambrai. At Monchy, with extreme bravery in dire circumstances, remnants of the badly mauled battalion eventually repulsed the overwhelming German counterattack and maintained their hold on the town in the face of ferocious fighting. In that action, the Essex lost 17 officers and 644 other ranks, killed, wounded or missing.

The battalion crossed the Steenbeek Canal in mid-August and captured Langemarke by 18th August but their losses of 235 were second only to those at 4th Krithia in the Gallipoli Peninsula. At the Battle of Cambrai in November the battalion was in the vanguard of the historic tank attack on the Hindenburg Line at Masnières Bridge. After a hold-up by sniper fire a battalion party crossed at nightfall and cleared them enabling the advance to continue.

In February 1918, the Battalion was at Passchendaele when a reorganisation of regiments meant they were transferred to 112th Brigade of 37th Division. They had served in 88th Brigade of the *"Incomparable 29th"* from formation in 1914 and featured in all the key battles from Gallipoli to Cambrai. General de Lisle wrote to Lt-Col Stirling expressing regret at losing *"a fine battalion."* They continued fighting with their new brigade throughout the last year of the war taking part in the last action at Sambre, on 5th November a week before the Armistice. (For more details of these actions see the relevant discussions.)

1919-1939

The 1st Battalion returned home in May 1919 and a colour party went to Paris for the Victory march on 14th July. They were then posted to active service in Ireland in August that year being stationed at Bandon and Kinsale to combat the IRA rebels in Cork up to independence in 1922, whence they were transferred to Carrickfergus, near Belfast in the new Northern Ireland.

After Ireland there was a stint with the League of Nations Peacekeeping force in the Saarland Plebiscite in the winter of 1934-35. This was necessary because of Nazi party agitation for reunion with Germany and indeed over 90% voted for that option in January 1935.

1939-1958

The battalion went to Palestine (1937-38) and was in Eygpt at the outbreak of WW2 in 1939. It served in the Middle East, Sudan, Iraq, Syria, Tobruk, Assam and Burma. Notably, it was involved in the successful break-out from Tobruk in November 1941, and the dangerous expeditions with Major General Orde Wingate's 'Chindits' behind the Japanese lines in Assam and Burma in 1944.

After the war, the 1st was amalgamated with the 2nd to form a new 1st Battalion (44th and 56th), while the need for anti-aircraft units in the re-formed Territorial Army meant that the 4th Battalion was the only remaining Essex Territorial Army Infantry battalion.

The new 1st Battalion served in Korea (1953 to 1954) where large numbers of young National Service soldiers from Dagenham earned them a nickname: "*The Dagenham Light Infantry*"!

It was then stationed in Hong Kong (1954-56) and was posted in West Germany from then onto 1958. On 2nd June 1958, while stationed at Dortmund, the 1st Battalion Essex Regiment was amalgamated with the 1st Battalion, Bedfordshire and Hertfordshire Regiment to form the 1st Battalion, the 3rd East Anglian Regiment.

This new regiment served in West Germany, in the Malayan Emergency, in Northern Ireland in a then peaceful time, before being posted to Berlin soon after the erection of the Berlin Wall in 1961. Whilst there, in September 1964, the regiments of the East Anglian Brigade were reconstituted into the first of the 'large regiments', being re-designated as the 3rd Battalion, The Royal Anglian Regiment. As that regiment they continued to serve in various parts: Aden (now Yemen), for an Emergency Tour in 1966, Aldershot, Cyprus, as part of UN forces, and Germany again, as part of the British Army of the Rhine (BAOR).

The 3rd Battalion, Royal Anglian Regiment served a number of tours in Northern Ireland between 1972 and 1992, in both rural and urban areas. Whilst on an operational tour there the Battalion learnt it was to be disbanded as part of cuts forced on the Army by the Government's 'Options for Change' paper.

On 5th October 1992 the 3rd Battalion, Royal Anglian Regiment (Bedfordshire, Hertfordshire and Essex), was disbanded at Colchester and its traditions and personnel were passed on to the 1st Battalion of the Regiment.

Despite modernisation it is still sad that a fine regiment with a distinguished history such as this should have to be subsumed within larger units. However, all the relatives of those who served will never forget their magnificent contribution at key points along the extended track of British military history.

On the Essex Regiment website it concludes: *"In all its long and colourful history The Essex Regiment has never failed in peace and war. It has only one standard in barracks or in battle – the highest. To attain this standard it must cling at all times to the old simple ideas that have made the British Army famous in history throughout the world – obedience, service and sacrifice."*

The men of Essex always served with dedication and distinction in whatever conditions they found themselves in and to whatever task they were ordered and were regularly complimented for their bravery and doggedness by all their Divisional and Brigade Commanders. In the Forward to Burrows' (1923) General Sir Ian Hamilton, who oversaw the action at Gallipoli, said of the Essex: *"Time and time again I have borne testimony to that calm fearlessness which is their distinctive trait in battle."*

Let us never forget them and continue to honour their service to our country.

NOTES

1. This quote is from Volume 3, *History of the War in South Africa* by Leo Amery, later a school contemporary of Churchill and Conservative politician and minister.

Sources

Baker, Chris (2002) *The Long, Long Trail: The British Army in the Great War*, www.1914-1918.net
This site proves useful in covering many aspects of the war and provides a handy context.

Barry, Tom (1949), *Guerrilla days in Ireland*, Dublin: Irish Press Ltd

Broadbent, Harvey (2005), *Gallipoli: The Fatal Shore*, London: Viking Books
Greater attention is given to the British landings and also with a useful Turkish perspective. No mention of 1st Essex though.

Buchan, John (1915), *The Thirty Nine Steps*, Edinburgh: William Blackwood & Sons. www.enwikipedia.org
He called it a 'shocker' namely an unlikely but just believable story here about a secret German plot to obtain Britain's war plans just in 1914.

Burrows, John William (1923), *1st Battalion, The Essex Regiment 1914-18*, Southend-on-Sea: John Burrows & Sons Ltd
The title confuses because the first half addresses the battalion's formation in 1740 and the major campaigns until 1914. The second half is a detailed focus on the battalion's movements during WW1.

Cave, Nigel (2003), *Beaumont Hamel (Somme)*, Barnsley: Pen & Sword Books
This chronological account of the first day in the north sector also acts as a detailed guide for Battlefield tourists.

Chesney, Captain George, May 1871, 'The Battle of Dorking', *Blackwood Magazine*, London: William Blackwood & Sons. www.britannica.com/EBchecked/topic/1055146/The-Battle-of-Dorking.
Lively and widely read novel about a German invasion of England after the Prussian victory over France. This article initiated the invasion genre in literature.

Essex Chronicle, Mentioned in Dispatch, 25th May 1917
"Mentioned by Field Marshal Sir Douglas Haig for distinguished and gallant services and devotion to duty: QSM & Hon Lt F Bailey"

Essex Chronicle, Essex Soldiers Honoured, 23rd July 1917
"Conferred by the King of Serbia: Cross of Karageorge, 1st Class (With Swords), Regimental Sergeant Major Frank Bailey Essex Regiment"

Fox, Colin (2000), *Monchy-le-Preux (Arras)*, Barnsley: Leo Cooper, Pen & Sword Books
A detailed account dedicated to his father who served there and featuring the significant contribution of 1st Essex.

Gillam, Major John (1918), *Gallipoli Diary*, London: Allen & Unwin
This first-hand diary of the campaign features the 1st Battalion Essex Regiment in action on the first day and throughout the campaign. It is available for reference at the IWM.

Gillon, Captain Stair (1925), *Story of the 29th Division: A record of gallant deeds*, London: Thomas Nelson
This is an interesting account of the men widely known and respected as "The Incomparable 29th". It is available for reference at the IWM.

Gough, Paul (2004), 'Sites in the imagination: the Beaumont Hamel Newfoundland Memorial on the Somme, *Cultural Geographies*, Vol. 11 No.2, Oxford: Blackwell

Griffith, Kenneth and O'Grady, Timothy (1998), *John L O'Sullivan, Curious Journey: An Oral History of Ireland's Unfinished Revolution*, Cork: Mercier Press

Haythornthwaite, Philip (2000), *Gallipoli 1915*, Oxford: Osprey Publishing

Holmes, Richard (2002), *Redcoat: The British soldier in the age of horse and musket*, London: Harper Collins. www.guardian.co.uk/books/2001/nov/03/historybooks.
This account of the period complements the larger background by the insertion of some aptly chosen graphic anecdotal evidence.

Holt, Tonie & Holt, Valmai (2000), *Gallipoli*, Barnsley: Leo Cooper
This is a battlefield guide book but contains much useful historical data as well.
Howard, Michael (2003), *The First World War*, Oxford: Oxford University Press. www.oup.com/uk/catalogue

Liddell Hart, Basil (1970), *History of the First World War*, Bath: Chivers

Martin, Colonel T.A. *The Essex Regiment 1929-1950*, Brentwood: Essex Regiment Association

Men of the 37th (1919), *The Golden Horseshoe: Journal of the 37th Division of the BEF*, London: Cassell & Co.

Middlebrook, Martin (2007), *The First Day on the Somme*, London: Pen & Sword Books Ltd
Inspired by a visit to the battlefields in 1967, this is a masterly piece of primary and secondary research of the first day of the British Army's costliest losses. No mention of 1st Essex at Beaumont Hamel.

Nicholls, Jonathan (1990), *Cheerful Sacrifice: Battle of Arras 1917*, Lee Cooper, Pen & Sword Books. www.pen-and-sword.co.uk

Rhodes James, Robert (1999), *Gallipoli*, London: Pimlico.
www.en.wikipedia.org/wiki/Robert Rhodes James
This detailed and balanced study is recognised as a definitive account.

Sheffield, Gary (2002), *Forgotten Victory -The First World War: myths and realities*, London: Review
This is a well-balanced analysis that objectively revises the myths of WW1 that pervade our public consciousness.

Spencer, William (2001), *Army Service Records of the First World War*, Richmond: Public Record Office

Stevenson, David (2004), *The History of the First World War*, London: Penguin Books
The Eagle, Journal of the Essex Regiment, Vol. XVI, No. 88: 249, May 1956
This is an appreciation by Brigadier Frederick Clarke, DSO, who served as Lieutenant with the battalion in Ireland during 1919-22

The Essex Regiment Gazette (1937), Depot Notes and News: Editorial, Vol. VI, No. 45, December
This is a valedictory summary of the regimental career of Major F Bailey, DCM.

The War Office, Supplement, *The London Gazette*, 4th March 1918: 2732
Citation: *Sergeant Major F Bailey, Essex Regiment, for "conspicuous gallantry and devotion to duty".*

Walker, Robert (1980), *Recipients of the DCM 1914-1920*, Birmingham: Midlands Medals. http://1914-1918.invisionzone.com/forums/lofiversion/index.php/t51706.html
This lists all the DCMs both regimentally and alphabetically awarded between August 1914 and June 1920.

Western Front Association (1921), *Men of Essex, The 1st Battalion The Essex Regiment 1914-1921*, Volume 7, Chelmsford, Essex Branch

Westlake, Ray (1994), *British Battalions on the Somme*, London: Pen & Sword Books Ltd

www.1914-18.net/diaries/wardiary-/Essex

www.measuringworth.com/ukcompare

The Western Front Association

(Registered Charity No. 298365)

The Western Front Association is the UK's leading educational and research charity dealing with all aspects of the First World War.

A nationwide branch network organises lectures, battlefield tours, museum visits, school competitions, commemorations, and research support for projects including family history.

Members, nearly 6,000 in 2011, receive the thrice-yearly journals *Stand To!*, containing historical articles, and *The Bulletin*, dealing with First World War related news and branch events.

Our website contains articles about the Great War, Association news and events, a discussion forum and a schools' section.

For an application form, please visit www.westernfrontassociation.com or write to: The Western Front Association, PO Box 1918, Stockport, Cheshire, SK4 4WN - Telephone 0161 443 1918